THE COMPLETE COOKBOOK FOR BEGINNERS

EASY RECIPES AND MEALS FOR EFFORTLESS EVERYDAY COOKING

© **Copyright 2021 - All rights reserved**.

This document is geared towards providing exact and reliable information in regard to the topic and issue covered.

- From a Declaration of Principles which was accepted and approved equally by a Committee of the American Bar Association and a Committee of Publishers and Associations.

In no way is it legal to reproduce, duplicate, or transmit any part of this document in either electronic means or in printed format. All rights reserved.

The information provided herein is stated to be truthful and consistent, in that any liability, in terms of inattention or otherwise, by any usage or abuse of any policies, processes, or directions contained within is the solitary and utter responsibility of the recipient reader. Under no circumstances will any legal responsibility or blame be held against the publisher for any reparation, damages, or monetary loss due to the information herein, either directly or indirectly.

Respective authors own all copyrights not held by the publisher.

The information herein is offered for informational purposes solely and is universal as so. The presentation of the information is without contract or any type of guarantee assurance.

The trademarks that are used are without any consent, and the publication of the trademark is without permission or backing by the trademark owner. All trademarks and brands within this book are for clarifying purposes only and are owned by the owners themselves, not affiliated with this document.

TABLE OF CONTENTS

INTRODUCTION ... 11
History of Sous Vide ... 11

CHAPTER 1. LIST OF THE NUTRITIONAL BENEFITS ON THE FOODS ... 13
Nutritional Benefits ... 13

CHAPTER 2. THE ADVANTAGES IN LIFE, LIKE MORE TIME ... 15
The Best Way to Cook Everything ... 15
The Advantages of Sous Vide ... 15
The Health Benefits of Sous Vide Cooking ... 16

CHAPTER 3. EQUIPMENT AND TOOLS NEEDED TO COOK ... 17
Anova Wi-Fi Precision Cooker ... 17
Chef Steps Joule ... 18
Gourmia Sous Vide Pod ... 18
A Reasonably Large Container ... 18
Resealable Bags and Jars ... 18
Cast Iron Pan ... 18
The Basics of Using the Sous Vide ... 19

CHAPTER 4. TIPS TO SAVE THE FOOD ... 20
What Is Sous Vide Cooking? ... 20
Steps to Safer Sous Vide Cooking ... 20
- *Always Use Pasteurized Eggs* ... 20
- *Only Use the Right Sous Vide Cookers* ... 20
- *Clean Your Sous Vide Cooking Equipment Properly* ... 21
- *Keep Your Sous Vide Equipment Dry* ... 21
- *Be Careful When Using Sous Vide Cookers* ... 21
- *Turn the Cooking Temperature Down* ... 21
- *Store Your Sous Vide Equipment in the Freezer or Refrigerator* ... 21
- *Take Precautions with Raw Seafood and Poultry* ... 21
- *Always Use a Meat Thermometer* ... 22
- *Take Precautions When Using Sous Vide Cookers* ... 22

CHAPTER 5.   BREAKFAST RECIPES 23
1.   OVERNIGHT OATMEAL 23
2.   OVERNIGHT OATMEAL WITH STEWED FRUIT COMPOTE 24
3.   FRENCH TOAST 25
4.   PERFECT EGG TOSTADA 26
5.   POACHED EGGS IN HASH BROWN NESTS 27
6.   SOUS VIDE MUSHROOMS 29
7.   SOUS VIDE CORN 30
8.   MEATBALLS 31
9.   TOMATO SUSHI 33
10.   FRESH VEGETABLES CONFIT 35
11.   EGGS AND OREGANO 36
12.   COCONUT & ALMOND PORRIDGE 37
13.   HUEVOS RANCHEROS 38
14.   SAUSAGE TOMATO 39
15.   PORRIDGE WITH CHIA AND FLAX SEEDS 40
16.   BAR-STYLE PINK PICKLED EGGS 41
17.   SHRIMP AND MUSHROOMS 42

CHAPTER 6.   LUNCH 43
18.   MIXED VEGETABLES 43
19.   BUTTERY MAPLE CARROTS 45
20.   BACON ASPARAGUS 46
21.   BUTTER-GLAZED SWEET POTATOES 47
22.   FINGERLING POTATOES WITH ROSEMARY 48
23.   SESAME EGGPLANT 49
24.   MAPLE BUTTERNUT SQUASH 50
25.   ZUCCHINI MEDALLIONS 51
26.   GARLICKY RATATOUILLE 52
27.   BACON-BRUSSELS SPROUTS 53
28.   CIDER DIPPED FENNEL 54
29.   GARLIC BROCCOLI 55
30.   LEMON-BUTTER SHRIMP 56

CHAPTER 7.   DINNER RECIPES 57

   31.   Tender Pork Chops 57
   32.   Pork Chops with Mushrooms 58
   33.   Pork Tenderloin 59
   34.   Herb Rub Pork Chops 60
   35.   Bone-In Pork Chop 61
   36.   Pork Loin 62
   37.   Lemon Pork Chops 63
   38.   BBQ Pork Ribs 64
   39.   Five-Spice Pork 65
   40.   BBQ Baby Back Ribs 66
   41.   Pork Carnitas 67
   42.   Pulled Pork 68
   43.   Simple Sliced Pork Belly 69
   44.   Perfect Pork Chop 70
   45.   Sweet and Spicy Pork Ribs 71
   46.   Rosemary Garlic Lamb Chops 72

CHAPTER 8.   RED MEATS 73

   47.   Simple Rack of Lamb 73
   48.   Herb Garlic Lamb Chops 74
   49.   Boneless Strip Steak 75
   50.   Korean Kalbi Short Ribs 76
   51.   Hanger Steak 77
   52.   Spice-Rubbed Short Ribs 78
   53.   Beef Shogayaki 79
   54.   Beef Meatballs 80
   55.   Roast Beef 81
   56.   Tuscan Rib Eye Steak 82
   57.   Burgers 83
   58.   Smoked Brisket 84
   59.   Spice-Rubbed BBQ Baby Back Ribs 85

CHAPTER 9.   VEGETABLE RECIPES 86

60.	Snow Peas with Mint	86
61.	Herbed Asparagus Mix	87
62.	Balsamic Braised Cabbage	88
63.	Nuts, Beetroot & Cheese Salad	89
64.	Creamy Cauliflower Broccoli Soup	90
65.	Mediterranean Eggplant Lasagna	91
66.	Traditional Ratatouille	92
67.	Speedy Poached Tomatoes	93
68.	Chili Brussels Sprouts in Sweet Syrup	94
69.	Aromatic Braised Beetroots	95
70.	Pomodoro Soup	96
71.	Simple Mushroom Soup	97
72.	Easy Mixed Vegetable Soup	98
73.	Power Green Soup	99
74.	Simple Hard-Boiled Eggs	100
75.	Colorful Bell Pepper Mix	101
76.	Cilantro Curried Zucchinis	102
77.	Paprika Bell Pepper Puree	103
78.	Artichoke Hearts with Green Chilies	104
79.	Chili & Garlic Sauce	105
80.	Parmesan Garlic Asparagus	106
81.	Blackened Brussels Sprouts with Garlic and Bacon	107
82.	Asian Inspired Bok Choy	108
83.	Rosemary and Garlic Potatoes	109
84.	Canded Sweet Potatoes	110

CHAPTER 10.   EGG RECIPES 111

85.	Smoked Fish and Poached Egg	111
86.	Brioche and Eggs	112
87.	Egg Bites	113
88.	Sous Vide Scrambled Eggs	114
89.	Egg with Sunchokes Velouté, Crispy Prosciutto and Hazelnut	115
90.	Sausage Scramble	117
91.	Eggs Benedict	118

CHAPTER 11. APPETIZER AND SNACK RECIPES 119

92. Buffalo Chicken Wings 119
93. Honey Garlic Chicken Wings 120
94. Hummus 121
95. Baba Ghanouj 122
96. White Bean and Artichoke Dip 123
97. Shrimp and Avocado Salsa 124
98. Tomato and Mango Salsa 125
99. Shrimp and Jalapeño Quesadilla 126
100. Deep-Fried Pork Belly Skewers with Honey Garlic Glaze 127
101. Tomato Confit and Provolone Grilled Cheese Sandwich Wedges 128
102. Flank Steak, Apricot, and Brie Bites 130
103. Pork Tenderloin, Tomato, and Bocconcini Canapés 131
104. Green Bean Almandine 132
105. Honey Ginger Carrots 133
106. Mashed Potatoes 134
107. Maple Butternut Squash Purée 135
108. Leek and Cauliflower Purée 136
109. Szechuan Broccoli 137
110. Buttered Corn on the Cob 138
111. Ratatouille 139
112. Sous-Vide Mashed Potatoes 140
113. A Bed of Vegetables Sous Vide 141
114. Sauerkraut 142
115. Asparagus 143
116. Hollandaise Sauce 144
117. Rosemary Potatoes 145
118. Hokkaido Pumpkin 146
119. Napkin Dumplings 147
120. Carrot Sticks 148
121. Sous-Vide Bolognese Sauce for Spaghetti 149

CHAPTER 12. SOUP AND STEW RECIPES 150

122.	Cream of Celery Soup	150
123.	Carrot & Coriander Soup	151
124.	Spring Onion Soup	152
125.	Chicken & Vegetable Soup	153
126.	Cauliflower Soup	154
127.	Butternut Squash & Apple Soup	155
128.	Chicken Noodle Soup	156
129.	Borscht	157
130.	Creamy Tomato Soup	158
131.	Chilled Pea & Cucumber Soup	159
132.	Slow Chicken Stock	160
133.	Sous Vide Cornish Hen Soup	161
134.	Chicken Curry Soup	162
135.	Stracciatella alla Romana Soup	164
136.	Oyster Stew	165
137.	Chicken Stock	166
138.	Spring Minestrone Soup	167
139.	Mushroom Orzo Green Soup	168
140.	Squash and Lentil Stew	169

CHAPTER 13.   DESSERT RECIPES 170

141.	Buttered Spiced Apples	170
142.	Strawberries	171
143.	Red Wine Poached Pears	172
144.	Rose Water Apricots	173
145.	Dolce De Leche	174
146.	Champagne Zabaglione	175
147.	Mexican Pot De Crème	176
148.	Lavender Spiced Crème Brulée	177
149.	Crème Brulée	178
150.	Leche Flan	179
151.	Cinnamon Clove Banana Bowls	180
152.	Creamy Sweet Corn Cheesecake	181
153.	Sweet Corn Cheesecake	182

154.	Bananas Foster	183
155.	Maple Raisin Rice Pudding with Ginger	184

CONCLUSION **185**

INTRODUCTION

So, you've heard about sous vide, the secret tool that everyone from Michelin-starred chefs to your local Food Network enthusiast swears by. Maybe you'd like to start Sous viding in your kitchen. Before you start, though, let's clear up the meaning of those two odds, hard-to-spell words. Sous vide (pronounced "soo veed") is a French term that translates to "under vacuum." Don't imagine sticking your steaks under a rumbling hoover, though—here; vacuum refers to vacuum sealing. The sous vide method of cooking involves placing food in a vacuum-sealed pouch, placing it in a water bath or a steamer, and cooking it at a relatively low temperature for a long, long time. This method allows unparalleled precision, so your food is always evenly cooked, juicy, and tender.

HISTORY OF SOUS VIDE

The seed of sous vide was planted as early as 1799 when the British colonel-scientist Sir Benjamin Thompson wrote about a way to cook vacuum-sealed foods in a kind of oven. The technology was there, but the method didn't gather steam until the 1960s.

That decade was the height of the mid-century trend for perfectly engineered, futuristic food, and food scientists were clamoring to keep up with Americans' hunger for innovation. When French and American food scientists first started experimenting with the sous vide method, though, they had long-term food preservation in mind, not perfectly tender steaks. This was the Cold War, after all, when doomsdayers around the world were stocking their cellars with canned meat and beans in anticipation of total war.

It wasn't until the 1970s that sous vide shed its industrial, war-machine shackles and became an indispensable tool of haute cuisine. We can thank the French for that shift, of course. Georges Pralus, a chef at the venerable, Three-Michelin-starred Restaurant Troisgros in Roanne, France, was the first to apply sous vide to fine French cooking. According to the annals of history, the first foodstuff to which he applied the method was a chunk of foie gras, the fatty heart of French cuisine. If there's anything a French gourmand loves, it's a thick slice of fattened goose liver, but foie gras is prone to discoloration and an unfortunate loss of fat during the cooking process. When Pralus applied the sous vide method to his foie gras, however, it came out flawlessly colored, evenly cooked, and meltingly unctuous, with barely a drop of lost fat. "Eureka!" he must have cried (in French).

Since the 1970s, the sous vide method has spread from the hallowed halls of places like Restaurant Troisgros to the appliance aisles of your local hardware store and the kitchens of dedicated home cooks around the world. With tools becoming smaller and less expensive every day, there's never been a better time to hop on board the sous-vide bandwagon. We'll even teach you how to use the sous vide method using nothing more than the appliances you already have in your kitchen.

Generally speaking, the process of vacuum-sealing food to extend shelf life has been around for a long time. However, it didn't gain recognition as a cooking method before the 1940s. Even after that, it took a lot of experimentation before people started to place vacuum-sealed food in a pot full of boiling water to cook it!

Therefore, as a cooking method, the origin of the Sous Vide technique finds its roots in the mid-1970s, when Chef Georges Praulus tried to develop a cooking technology that would minimize costly shrinkage and help create an optimal cooking environment for cooking Foie Gras!

The technique of Sous Vide cooking was not confined to him. Soon after Praulus introduced the technique to the world, Chef Bruno Goussault took up the method and refined it further, which allowed him to use Sous Vide to craft meals for the first-class travelers of Air France!

Seeing the hidden potential behind the technique, Bruno worked relentlessly to bring the method to the mainstream market.

However, despite reaching mass popularity, it still was a costly technique for ordinary people to afford. It took two years of evolution before it completely broke the barriers and became one of the "Best" cooking technique ever made!

Contrary to popular belief, thanks to a large number of affordable Sous Vide circulators available in the market, anyone can pick up the device and start experimenting with Sous Vide cooking!

CHAPTER 1. LIST OF THE NUTRITIONAL BENEFITS ON THE FOODS

I have found that cooking food sous vide can be a great way to ensure a perfect, evenly cooked piece of meat. There are many different advantages of this cooking method, so I would like to introduce you to just a few of the nutritional benefits an individual may get from these foods.

Sous vide is essentially a French term that means "under vacuum." This differentiates it from other forms of braising and roasting by having the food put into sealed plastic bags and then cooked in water baths at low temperatures. Many people feel that this cooking method is more energy efficient because it cooks the food at a lower temperature for longer periods compared to other forms of cooking. Sous vide has been used in many different ways throughout history. In the 1800s, it was used as an inexpensive, rapid way to preserve meat. This was done by using salt and ice to prevent the growth of bacteria. Although sous vide has been used in many different ways, it is not a new concept. In fact, it has been around for centuries.

NUTRITIONAL BENEFITS

There are many different nutritional benefits that a person can get from sous vide cooking. Some of these benefits include the following:

- **Protein Promoter:** Sous vide cooking has been proven to increase the amount of protein in food. This helps fill you up more and can help keep you full for longer.

- **Healthy Fat:** Sous vide cooking can be a great way to get healthy fats into your diet. It is known to make the fat in the food greater and more evenly distributed, which can help lower the risk of high cholesterol levels.

- **Less Fattening:** Sous vide can be a great way to help people lose weight because of how much more evenly the food cooks. This means that there is less of a chance for it to burn or overcook.

- **Healthy Hydration:** Sous vide can help improve the level of hydration in your food. The food is cooked by being sealed in bags, which are then sprayed with water. This helps increase the amount of water that is retained in the food.

- **Meatier:** Sous vide cooking has been proven to cause a meatier flavor in the food. This is because it can help break down collagen, which is what gives meat that chewy texture.
- **Cooking Analysis:** Sous vide cooking has been proven to be more effective in ensuring the safety of fattier foods and allowing for more precise temperatures.

Sous vide cooking is a great way to ensure the healthiest cut of meat. It is also a great way to ensure that the taste and texture of the meat have been properly taken care of. This is important because people who choose to eat healthy meats have to make sure that they are getting their money's worth. One can only benefit from sous vide cooking if they know what foods they should try this with.

The most important one of all is that there is no worry about overcooking the food, which means that the food won't lose all of its moisture or taste. This allows for a more natural mouth feel and taste because only as much as you want to eat will be there. Another benefit that comes with sous vide cooking is the tenderness of the meat because it will be cooked evenly, leaving less room for error. This means that it won't be dried out. Also, sous vide allows for a great deal of versatility and creativity in its cooking. Some people like to cook their vegetables through this method by putting them into bags and then putting these bags alongside their meats to cook both at the same time without any worry about one taking over the other.

Although many benefits come from sous vide cooking, there are some that I feel that it should be taken into consideration for people who want to improve their health. For example, one of the most important ones is the fact that sous vide cooking uses less fat than other forms of cooking. Personally, this is something that I have a lot of interest in since I'm watching my fat intake. Sous vide also allows for a much higher level of moisture in food. Since sous vide cooks at lower temperatures, it won't risk drying any of the protein out. Finally, because there is no worry about overcooking the food, it won't be harmful to your health.

CHAPTER 2. THE ADVANTAGES IN LIFE, LIKE MORE TIME

Sous vide is a cooking technique that allows people to make unbelievably tender and juicy meats. It also gives people the ability to cook perfect desserts and vegetables every time. In this blog post, we are going to go over some of the advantages of sous vide so that you can understand why it's such a great way to cook.

THE BEST WAY TO COOK EVERYTHING

I get asked a lot what my favorite sous vide method is. My short answer is that I love them all. The thing is, though, if I had to choose one, it would have to be the immersion circulator. I've cooked with the best gas, electric, and braiser circulators, and the immersion circulator is hands down my favorite. Out of all of the sous vide methods, I find that sous vide is best for cooking meats because it allows you to control the temperature. This is important because when you cook meat for too long, it becomes tough and chewy instead of juicy and tender. The sous vide method allows you to set the temperature to whatever you want between 130 and 145 degrees Fahrenheit.

If you decide to cook in a slow cooker, oven, or even on the stove, then it's difficult to control the temperature of the food as it cooks. Choosing one of those cooking methods means that you'll have to constantly check and adjust your heat to keep your food from burning.

THE ADVANTAGES OF SOUS VIDE

The following advantages should inspire you to jump onto the Sous Vide bandwagon!

- It will allow you to create perfect meals every single time, regardless of your cooking experience.
- It will help you infuse your meals with "Gourmet" quality flavors and enjoy restaurant-quality meals at home.
- You do not need to stand in front of the water bath all day long, saving you a lot of time to carry out your day-to-day activities.
- The natural juices and nutrients are preserved in Sous Vide cooking.

- Since there's no risk of overcooking or undercooking, you will be able to cook your expensive meat cuts with ease!
- It will help you maintain the moisture in your meat cuts, making them always tender and juicy.
- It will be a wholesome way of cooking because you don't have to carry out the meat on a plate after it has been cooked.
- You can cook at home without spending tons of money on expensive meats.

THE HEALTH BENEFITS OF SOUS VIDE COOKING

While the advantages mentioned above focused on the general aspects of Sous Vide, the following will provide you with a detailed outline of the health benefits of accompanying Sous Vide.

- While cooking with Sous Vide devices, you won't need to add any additional fats needed in other methods. This immediately eliminates the need for using harmful oils that increase the cholesterol levels of the food, making Sous Vide meals much healthier.
- Exposing ingredients to heat, oxygen, and water causes them to lose a lot of vital nutrients, leading to over-carbonization of meats and vitamin/antioxidant loss in vegetables. The vacuum sealing technique implemented while cooking with Sous Vide prevents this from happening, as the food is not exposed to any water or oxygen. As a result, the nutritional contents are preserved to near-perfect levels.
- Sous Vide cooked meals are easier to digest, as it helps to break down the collagen proteins into gelatin, which is easier for our body to digest and absorb.
- Undercooking is very harmful, as it not only leads to unpleasant tasting food but also causes the foods to be overrun by bacteria and viruses. The vacuum seal of Sous Vide prevents this from happening, and the oxygen required for the pathogens to live is sucked out. The precise cooking technique ensures that you are getting perfectly cooked meals every single time.

CHAPTER 3. EQUIPMENT AND TOOLS NEEDED TO COOK

While it is true that Uber-expensive equipment is available that would allow you to create even more "premium" meals; it is still possible to achieve the same level of satisfaction without burning a hole in your pocket.

Thanks to technological advancements, Sous Vide circulators have become very cheap and affordable (you can get some good ones for as low as 60$!), which makes it easier for the mainstream market to penetrate Sous Vide cooking.

Aside from the circulator itself, you need a few other pieces of equipment, which are easily available for low prices in the supermarket or can even be found at your home!

I will be talking about all of them in a bit, but before that, let me talk a bit about the Sous Vide Circulator itself.

The Sous Vide Immersion Circulator: The Sous Vide circulators are the heart of Sous Vide cooking.

The main purpose of these devices is to simply heat your water bath to a very specific temperature with utmost precision and maintain that specified temperature throughout the cooking process.

The circulator also circulates the water to ensure that the heat is distributed evenly.

If you are buying a Sous Vide circulator for the first time, though, the following are the best ones available right now!

ANOVA WI-FI PRECISION COOKER

The Anova Wi-Fi Circulator is the top dog in the Sous Vide business, and it took the world by storm when it launched. Aside from the obvious cooking functionality, other additional features, such as Bluetooth or Wi-Fi connectivity that allows wireless controlling, make this the complete package, perfect for beginners!

CHEF STEPS JOULE

While Anova is considered the leading device, the Chef Steps Joule is the pioneer when it comes to the "Smart Kitchen" scene! When this device was introduced, fans instantly fell in love with the device, thanks to its compact size and robust array of features.

GOURMIA SOUS VIDE POD

The Gourmia is the one to go for if you are on a tight budget! This Sous Vide circulator has all of the basic functionalities you would expect without letting go of the "Cool" aesthetics!

Aside from the circulator itself, the following are some of the other essential items you would need.

A REASONABLY LARGE CONTAINER

You should already know that you will need a good-quality container to prepare your water bath to submerge your vacuum-sealed container and cook the contents. Therefore, it is wise to go for a good quality 8-12-quart stockpot. However, if not possible, then you should go for a 12-quart square, polycarbonate food storage container, just to be safe. Either way, make sure to purchase a container that can hold water heated to 203 degrees Fahrenheit.

RESEALABLE BAGS AND JARS

Once you are set with the container, the next items you are going to need are the resealable bags and sealing jars.

When considering the bags, you should go for heavy-duty, resealable bags capable of sustaining a temperature of up to 195 degrees Fahrenheit. If possible, get bags that are marked "Freezer Safe" and come with a double seal.

For the jars, simply go for mason jars or canning jars that come with a tight lid.

You might notice that throughout the book, we used the "Immersion" method for sealing zip bags and the "Finger Tip Tight" technique for tightening cans; both of the techniques are explained below.

CAST IRON PAN

Some recipes will ask you to sear your meal after Sous Vide cooking is done, so keeping a Cast Iron Pan nearby is a good decision. Alternatively, you may also achieve a brown texture using a blowtorch.

THE BASICS OF USING THE SOUS VIDE

While some recipes will call for deviations in the process, the following are the basic steps you need to follow while cooking using the Sous Vide Device.

- **Prepare:** once you have decided which container to use, simply attach the Immersion Circulator to the container and fill it up with water. Make sure to keep the height of the water just 1 inch above the minimum watermark of the circulator that you are using.
  Dutch oven, plastic storage containers, stockpot, and large saucepans are good options for Sous Vide cooking.
- **Choose a Temperature:** set the temperature of your circulator as asked by your recipe.
- **Pre-heat Water Bath:** turn the device on and allow the water bath to reach the desired temperature; it should take about 20-30 minutes, depending on your device.
- **Season and Seal the Meal:** season your food as instructed by the recipe and vacuum seal it in either a zip bag or canning jars.
- **Submerge Underwater:** once the desired water level has been reached and sealed your bags, submerge the food underwater and cover the container with a plastic wrap.
- **Wait until Cooked:** wait until cooking is complete.
- **Add Some Finishing Touches:** take your bag out and follow the remaining recipes for some finishing touches!

CHAPTER 4. TIPS TO SAVE THE FOOD

Many chefs are switching to sous vide cooking for its convenience and safety. However, this method is not without its disadvantages or risks. This article will give you tips on how to safely sous vide that can help make your experience more enjoyable and limit the pitfalls of this cooking technique.

WHAT IS SOUS VIDE COOKING?

Sous vide, or vacuum packing, is a method of food preservation in which food is sealed in plastic bags with a vacuum sealer and then cooked in a water bath to the desired temperature. Sous vide cooking uses the same principle as regular frying: cooking in small batches at low temperatures to preserve the maximum amount of flavor and nutrients. Sous vide also offers many benefits for preparing foods at home, providing safe and consistent results every time.

STEPS TO SAFER SOUS VIDE COOKING

The benefits and pleasures of sous vide cooking are many, but many potential dangers can ruin a perfectly good meal. By following a few simple tips, you can ensure that your sous vide cooking is as safe and healthy as possible without compromising the taste. Here are some tips for avoiding mishaps while sous viding:

Always Use Pasteurized Eggs

Sous vide cooking tells us to use eggs heated to a minimum of 145 degrees for five minutes. Some people may want to cook the eggs longer because they want the yolk to be more solid. This is not advisable since doing so can raise the chance of bacteria growing inside the egg and making you sick. When you are going sous vide, always use pasteurized eggs to make sure that this does not happen.

Only Use the Right Sous Vide Cookers

Chefs also use sous vide cooking to cook food for long periods because it preserves the flavor and nutrients in food, giving you a more flavorful meal. However, this can only be done when you use the right cookers, such as sous vide immersion circulators. These cookers must be regularly cleaned and sanitized so that no harmful bacteria will grow in your cooker.

Clean Your Sous Vide Cooking Equipment Properly

When you are through with your sous vide cooking, you must take the time to clean your cooker thoroughly. Unlike normal cooking in a pot, there is no way to tell when bacteria will start growing in your sous vide cooker since it will be turned off. The only way to prevent bacteria from growing in there is by regularly rinsing it out with water and sanitizing it properly.

Keep Your Sous Vide Equipment Dry

When using sous vide cooker, every single piece of equipment must be kept completely dry. This will mean that you do not have to worry about bacteria growing inside your sous vide cooker since the only scary thing about it is the fact that it can get very hot during cooking.

Be Careful When Using Sous Vide Cookers

When you are using sous vide cooker, make sure that you do it in a very open space, away from kids or pets. The cooker can get very hot when in use and is not for children and pets because they can easily be burned by it. This means that you will need to use it in the kitchen or on your patio so that you can keep an eye on your cooking without running the risk of forgetting about it.

Turn the Cooking Temperature Down

It is always better to cook sous vide food at a lower temperature and then allow it to cool before serving it. This will ensure that not all the vitamins and flavors have been cooked out of your food simply because you have overcooked it.

Store Your Sous Vide Equipment in the Freezer or Refrigerator

Once you are done cooking, you should store your equipment in the freezer or refrigerator until you are ready to use it again. This will ensure that any bacteria have died and that you can safely use your sous vide cooker the next time.

Take Precautions with Raw Seafood and Poultry

When using sous vide cooking, it is best to cook seafood or poultry only for short periods to prevent bacteria from growing in your food.

Always Use a Meat Thermometer

Using a sous vide cooker does not mean that you do not have to use a meat thermometer. You should always take the time to use your meat thermometer to make sure that your food is cooked to the right temperature. This will prevent any burns or other issues from happening when you make mistakes with your sous vide cooking, making it safer for everyone around.

Take Precautions When Using Sous Vide Cookers

When you are using a sous vide cooker, always take the time to clean it properly. The food particles that have been in your cooker will start to grow bacteria if you do not do it every now and then. This means you should clean it thoroughly regularly and not when you see some dirt on it.

CHAPTER 5. BREAKFAST RECIPES

1. OVERNIGHT OATMEAL

Preparation Time: 11 minutes
Cooking Time: 10 hours
Serving: 4
Ingredients:
- 2/3 cup of rolled oats
- 2/3 cup of pinhead oatmeal
- 1 1/3 cups of milk or cream
- 4 teaspoons of raisins
- 2 cups of water

Directions:
1. Follow the instructions given in the manual and fill the sous vide water oven. Preheat it to 140 °F.
2. Take 4 Mason jars or glass jam jars with lids. Divide the oats and pinhead oatmeal (you can also use quick-cook steel-cut oats) among the jars. Divide the milk and pour it over the oats. Pour ½ cup of water into each jar.
3. Add a teaspoon of raisins to each jar. Fasten the lids lightly, not tight.
4. Immerse the filled jars in the water bath. The lids of the jars should be above the level of water in the cooker. This is important.
5. Set the timer for 9 to 10 hours.
6. When done, stir and serve with some butter, if desired.

Nutrition:
- Calories: 284
- Fat: 20 g
- Protein: 9 g

2. OVERNIGHT OATMEAL WITH STEWED FRUIT COMPOTE

Preparation Time: 9 minutes
Cooking Time: 6 hours
Serving: 4
Ingredients:
For the oatmeal:
- 2 cups of quick-cooking rolled oats
- ¼ teaspoon of ground cinnamon
- 6 cups of water
- A pinch of salt

For the Stewed Fruit Compote:
- 1 ½ cups of mixed dried fruit of your choice—cherries, apricots, cranberries, etc.
- 1 cup of water
- Zest of an orange, finely grated
- Zest of a lemon, finely grated
- ¼ cup of white sugar
- ¼ teaspoon of vanilla extract

Directions:
1. Follow the instructions given in the manual and fill the sous vide water oven. Preheat it to 155 °F.
2. Place the oatmeal, water, salt, and cinnamon in a vacuum-seal pouch or Ziploc bag.
3. Place all the ingredients of the fruit compote in another similar pouch, and vacuum seal both.
4. Submerge both pouches in the water bath and set the timer for 6 to 10 hours.
5. Remove the pouches and shake them well.
6. Divide the oatmeal into 4 bowls. Top with fruit compote and serve.

Nutrition:
- Calories: 364
- Fat: 32 g
- Protein: 19 g

3. FRENCH TOAST

Preparation Time: 13 minutes
Cooking Time: 60 minutes
Serving: 8
Ingredients:
- 8 slices of bread
- 1 cup of heavy cream
- 1 teaspoon of ground cinnamon
- 4 eggs
- 2 teaspoons vanilla extract

For finishing:
- ½ cup of butter

Directions:
1. Follow the instructions given in the manual and fill the sous vide water oven. Preheat it to 147 °F.
2. Add eggs, vanilla, cream, and cinnamon into a bowl and whisk well.
3. Dip the bread slices in the egg mixture, one at a time, and place in a large vacuum-seal pouch or Ziploc bag. Use 2 bags, if desired. Place in a single layer.
4. Vacuum seal the pouch.
5. Submerge the pouch in the water bath. Set the timer for 60 minutes.
6. Remove the pouch from the water bath and remove the bread slices from the pouch.
7. For finishing: Place a large skillet over medium heat.
8. Add 1 or 2 tablespoons butter. When butter melts, place 2 or 3 bread slices on the pan and cook to desired doneness.

Nutrition:
- Calories: 404
- Fat: 29 g
- Protein: 13 g

4. PERFECT EGG TOSTADA

Preparation Time: 13 minutes
Cooking Time: 16 minutes
Serving: 4
Ingredients:
- 4 large eggs, at room temperature
- ¼ cup of cooked or canned black beans, heated
- 4 corn tostadas
- 4 teaspoon of salsa taquera or salsa Verde or chili de árbol
- 4 teaspoons of fresh cheese, crumbled

Directions:
1. Follow the instructions given in the manual and fill the sous vide water oven. Preheat it to 162°F.
2. Place the eggs on a spoon, one at a time, gently lower them into the water bath, and place them on the rack. Set the timer for 15 minutes.
3. When the timer goes off, immediately remove the eggs from the water bath. Place the eggs in a bowl of cold water for a few minutes.
4. To assemble: Place the tostadas on 4 serving plates. Spread a tablespoon of beans over it, the salsa, then sprinkle cheese on top and serve.

Nutrition:
- Calories: 354
- Fat: 28 g
- Protein: 16 g

5. POACHED EGGS IN HASH BROWN NESTS

Preparation Time: 11 minutes
Cooking Time: 60 minutes
Serving: 3
Ingredients:
- 6 large eggs, at room temperature
- 3 cups of frozen shredded hash brown, thawed completely
- 1 teaspoon of fresh rosemary, chopped, or ¼ teaspoon dried rosemary
- Freshly ground pepper to taste
- Salt to taste
- 2 tablespoons of chopped fresh chives
- 1 ½ tablespoon of extra-virgin olive oil
- ¼ teaspoon of paprika
- 3 thin slices of prosciutto, halved crosswise
- Cooking spray

Directions:
1. Follow the instructions given in the manual and fill the sous vide water oven. Preheat it to 147 °F.
2. Place the eggs on a spoon, one at a time, gently lower them into the water bath, and place them on the lower rack. Set the timer for 60 minutes.
3. Meanwhile, grease a 6-count muffin pan with cooking spray.
4. Place hash browns on a kitchen towel. Squeeze out as much moisture as possible.
5. Place the hash browns in a bowl. Add oil, rosemary, pepper, paprika, and salt. Mix well.
6. Divide this mixture among the muffin cups. Press down at the bottom and sides of the muffin cups. Spray cooking spray over it.
7. Preheat oven to 375 °F.
8. Place the muffin tin in the oven and bake for about 30 minutes or until nearly golden brown.
9. Place half slice of prosciutto over each hash brown. Let it hang from the edges of the hash brown nests. Bake for 5 minutes.

10. Remove from the oven and cool for 4 or 5 minutes. Run a knife around the edges of the hash brown nest and gently lift it out from the muffin tin.
11. When the timer of the sous vide cooker goes off, immediately remove the eggs. Break 2 cooked eggs in each nest. Garnish with chives and serve immediately.

Nutrition:
- Calories: 384
- Fat: 27 g
- Protein: 19 g

6. SOUS VIDE MUSHROOMS

Preparation Time: 9 minutes
Cooking Time: 30 minutes
Serving: 8
Ingredients:
- 2 pounds of mushrooms of your choice
- 4 tablespoons of extra-virgin olive oil
- 4 teaspoons of minced fresh thyme
- 1 teaspoon of salt or to taste
- 1 teaspoon of freshly ground pepper, or to taste
- 4 tablespoons of soy sauce
- 2 tablespoons of vinegar of your choice

Directions:
1. Follow the instructions given in the manual and fill the sous vide water oven. Preheat it to 176°F.
2. Place the mushrooms in a bowl. Add the rest of the ingredients and stir until well coated.
3. Transfer into a large vacuum-seal pouch or Ziploc bag.
4. Vacuum seal the pouch.
5. Submerge the pouch in the water bath. Set the timer for 30 minutes.
6. When the timer goes off, remove the pouch from the water bath. Set aside to cool.
7. Open the pouch and transfer it into a bowl.
8. Serve right away.

Nutrition:
- Calories: 429
- Fat: 34 g
- Protein: 18 g

7. SOUS VIDE CORN

Preparation Time: 12 minutes
Cooking Time: 30 minutes
Serving: 2
Ingredients:
- 2 ears corn
- Kosher salt to taste
- 1 tablespoon of butter + extra to serve

Aromatics: (optional, to taste)
- Handful cilantro, chopped
- 1 or 2 scallions, chopped
- Dried red chilies to taste
- 4 or 5 cloves of garlic, minced

Directions:
1. Follow the instructions given in the manual and fill the sous vide water oven. Preheat it to 183 °F.
2. Add all the ingredients, including the aromatics, into a vacuum-seal pouch or Ziploc bag. Vacuum seal the pouch.
3. Submerge the pouch in the water bath and fix it on the edge of the water bath with clips.
4. Set timer for 30 minutes.
5. Remove corn from the pouch and discard the rest of the ingredients.
6. Brush with more butter and serve.

Nutrition:
- Calories: 244
- Fat: 27 g
- Protein: 13 g

8. MEATBALLS

Preparation Time: 9 minutes

Cooking Time: 3 hours

Serving: 10

Ingredients:

- 2 pounds of ground beef
- 4 to 6 ounces of milk
- ½ teaspoon of pepper
- 1 shallot minced
- 2 tablespoons of dried oregano
- 6 tablespoons of grated parmesan cheese
- ½ cup of dried breadcrumbs
- 1 teaspoon of salt, or to taste
- 2 large eggs, beaten
- 1/3 cup of chopped parsley
- 2 tablespoons of garlic powder
- Dip of your choice, to serve

- A little oil to seas (optional)

Directions:
1. Add all the ingredients into a large bowl and mix with your hands until just incorporated. Do not mix for long, as the meat will tend to get tough.
2. Make 1-inch balls of the mixture. Place on a tray and freeze until firm.
3. Follow the instructions given in the manual and fill the sous vide water oven. Preheat it to 135 °F.
4. Transfer the meatballs into 1 or 2 large vacuum-seal pouches or Ziploc bags.
5. Vacuum seal the pouches.
6. Immerse the pouches in the water bath. Set the timer for 3 hours.
7. When the timer goes off, remove the pouch from the water bath. Set aside to cool.
8. Open the pouch and transfer it into a bowl.
9. Serve with a dip of your choice.
10. If you want to sear the meatballs: Place a non-stick pan over medium heat and add a bit of oil. When the oil is heated, add meatballs and cook until browned.
11. Serve.

Nutrition:
- Calories: 417
- Fat: 21 g
- Protein: 17 g

9. TOMATO SUSHI

Preparation Time: 7 minutes
Cooking Time: 30 minutes
Serving: 24
Ingredients:
For the tomatoes:
- 6 Roma tomatoes
- 2 tablespoons of soy sauce
- 2 cups of water
- 6 nori sheets
- ½ teaspoon of salt

For the sushi rice:
- 2 cups of uncooked glutinous white rice, rinsed
- ½ cup of rice vinegar
- ½ teaspoon of salt
- 3 cups of water
- 4 tablespoons of sugar

Directions:
For the tomatoes:
1. Follow the instructions given in the manual and fill the sous vide water oven. Preheat it to 140 °F.
2. Add 4 nori sheets, soy sauce, water, and salt in a large saucepan over medium heat.
3. Simmer until it has reduced to half its original quantity. Turn off the heat.
4. Cut off a slice from the top of the tomatoes. Make cuts in the shape of an "X" with a paring knife.
5. Place a pan with water over high heat. When it begins to boil, add the tomatoes and let it cook for about 30 to 60 seconds. Remove the tomatoes and place them in a bowl filled with ice and water.
6. Peel the tomatoes. Cut each into quarters. Discard the seeds.

7. Place the tomatoes in the nori water. Transfer into a vacuum-seal pouch or Ziploc bag. Vacuum seal the pouch.
8. Submerge the pouch in a water bath and adjust the timer for 4 hours.

<u>To make the sushi rice:</u>
9. Add vinegar, salt, and sugar into a saucepan over medium heat. Stir frequently until sugar dissolves. Turn off the heat.
10. Add rice and water into a pot over high heat. When it begins to boil, reduce the heat and cover it with a lid. Simmer until all liquid is absorbed.
11. Add sugar solution and mix well. Turn off the heat.

<u>To assemble:</u>
12. Cut the remaining nori sheets into 24 strips. Remove the pouch from the water bath.
13. When the rice is cool enough to handle, divide the rice into 24 equal portions and shape it into sushi.
14. Place a piece of tomato on each sushi. Wrap the sushi along with the tomato with a nori strip and place it on a serving platter.
15. Serve.

Nutrition:
- Calories: 514
- Fat: 36 g
- Protein: 19 g

10. FRESH VEGETABLES CONFIT

Preparation Time: 8 minutes
Cooking Time: 2 hours
Serving: 10
Ingredients:
- 1 cup of peeled pearl onions
- 1 cup of peeled garlic cloves
- 6 cups of olive oil
- 2 cups of halved, deseeded mini peppers

Garnish:
- 10 to 12 ounces of spreadable goat cheese
- Ciabatta bread slices, as required, toasted
- Salt to taste
- Fresh herbs of your choice

Directions:
1. Follow the instructions given in the manual and fill the sous vide water oven. Preheat it to 185 °F.
2. Place garlic in a Ziploc bag or vacuum-seal pouch. Pour 1½ cups of oil into the pouch.
3. Add the mini peppers into a second Ziploc bag. Pour 3 cups of oil into the pouch.
4. Add the pearl onions into a third Ziploc bag. Pour 1½ cups of oil into the pouch.
5. Vacuum seal the pouches.
6. Immerse the pouches in a water bath and adjust the timer for 1½ hours. When the timer goes off, remove the pouches from the water bath and place them in chilled water for 30 minutes.
7. Spread the goat cheese over toasted ciabatta slices. Top with vegetables from each pouch. Garnish with fresh herbs and serve.

Nutrition:
- Calories: 387
- Fat: 31 g
- Protein: 19 g

11. EGGS AND OREGANO

Preparation Time: 9 minutes
Cooking Time: 32 minutes
Serving: 2
Ingredients:
- 1 red bell pepper, chopped
- 2 shallots, chopped
- 4 eggs, whisked
- A pinch of salt and black pepper
- 1 tablespoon of oregano, chopped
- ½ teaspoon of chili powder
- ½ teaspoon of sweet paprika

Directions:
1. Prepare your Sous-vide water bath to a temperature of 170 °F.
2. Pour the whisked eggs into a cooking pouch and add the other ingredients.
3. Immerse the pouch into the water bath and cook for 30 minutes.
4. Once done, remove the pouch from the water bath and transfer the contents to a serving plate.
5. Serve and enjoy!

Nutrition
- Calories: 331
- Fat: 7 g
- Protein: 7 g

12. COCONUT & ALMOND PORRIDGE

Preparation Time: 11 minutes
Cooking Time: 3 hours
Serving: 1
Ingredients:

- ½ cup of ground almonds
- ¾ cup of coconut cream
- 1 teaspoon of Cinnamon powder
- 1 teaspoon of Stevia
- 1 pinch of ground cardamom
- 1 pinch of ground cloves
- 1 pinch of Nutmeg

Directions:

1. Combine all of the ingredients in a vacuum-sealed bag.
2. Introduce the bag to the preheated water bath for 3 hours at 180 °F.
3. Remove from the bag, serve, and enjoy.

Nutrition:

- Calories: 260
- Fat: 12 g
- Protein: 16 g

13. HUEVOS RANCHEROS

Preparation Time: 11 minutes
Cooking Time: 2 hours 30 minutes
Serving: 3
Ingredients:
- ½ can (7 ounces) of crushed tomatoes
- ½ small yellow onion, minced
- 2 cloves of garlic, minced
- ¼ teaspoon of dried oregano
- ¼ teaspoon of ground cumin
- ½ lime juice
- 1 canned chipotle adobo chili, minced
- ½ can of refried beans
- 6 eggs
- 6 corn tortillas
- ¼ cup of fresh cilantro, chopped
- ½ cup of crumbled cotija cheese or grated Monterey Jack

Directions:
1. Preheat the water bath to 147 °F.
2. Combine the tomatoes, onion, garlic, oregano, cumin, lime, and chili in a bag. Seal using the water method.
3. Pour refried beans into a second bag and seal using the water method. Place eggs in a third bag and seal using the water method.
4. Place all three bags into the water bath. Cook for 2 hours.
5. When the other components have 20 minutes left to cook, heat tortillas in a pan. Place 2 on each plate.
6. Top the tortillas with salsa, followed by the shelled eggs, cheese, and cilantro. Serve with refried beans.

Nutrition:
- Calories: 554
- Fat: 34.6 g
- Protein: 28.5 g

14. SAUSAGE TOMATO

Preparation Time: 9 minutes
Cooking Time: 43 minutes
Serving: 4
Ingredients:

- 1 cup of baby spinach
- 1 tablespoon of avocado oil
- 2 pork sausage links, sliced
- 1 cup of cherry tomatoes, halved
- 1 cup of Kalamata olives, pitted and halved
- 2 tablespoons of lemon juice
- 2 tablespoons of basil pesto
- Salt and black pepper to the taste

Directions:

1. Prepare your sous vide water bath to a temperature of 180 °F.
2. Get a cooking pouch and add all the listed ingredients.
3. Immerse the pouch into the water bath and let it cook for 40 minutes.
4. Once done, remove the pouch from the water bath.
5. Transfer the contents into two serving bowls.
6. Serve and enjoy!

Nutrition:

- Calories: 250
- Fat: 12 g
- Protein: 18 g

15. PORRIDGE WITH CHIA AND FLAX SEEDS

Preparation Time: 11 minutes
Cooking Time: 3 hours 3 minutes
Serving: 1
Ingredients:

- 2 tablespoons of flax seeds
- 1 cup of almond milk
- 1 tablespoon of Stevia
- 1 tablespoon of Chia seeds
- ½ cup of hemp hearts
- ½ teaspoon of cinnamon powder
- ¾ teaspoon of vanilla extract
- ¼ cup of almond flour

Directions:

1. Prepare the water bath.
2. Combine all of the ingredients in a mixing container.
3. Pour into a vacuum-sealable baggie and cook for 3 hours (180 °F) in the prepared Sous Vide cooker.
4. Add to your plate and enjoy it.

Nutrition:

- Calories: 230
- Fat: 12 g
- Protein: 13 g

16. BAR-STYLE PINK PICKLED EGGS

Preparation Time: 6 minutes
Cooking Time: 2 hours 2 minutes
Serving: 6
Ingredients:

- 6 eggs
- 1 cup of white vinegar
- 1 can of beets Juice
- ¼ cup of sugar
- ½ tablespoon of salt
- 2 cloves of garlic
- 1 bay leaf

Directions:

1. Preheat the water bath to 170 °F.
2. Place the eggs in the bag. Seal the bag and place it in the water bath. Cook 1 hour.
3. After 1 hour, place eggs in the bowl of cold water to cool and carefully peel. In the bag in which you cooked the eggs, combine vinegar, beet juice, sugar, salt, garlic, and bay leaf.
4. Replace eggs in the bag with pickling liquid. Replace in the water bath and cook for 1 additional hour.
5. After 1 hour, move eggs with pickling liquid to the refrigerator. Allow cooling completely before eating.

Nutrition:

- Calories: 166
- Fat: 10 g
- Protein: 9.3 g

17. SHRIMP AND MUSHROOMS

Preparation Time: 11 minutes
Cooking Time: 30 minutes
Serving: 4
Ingredients:
- 1 cup of shrimp, peeled and deveined
- 3 spring onions, chopped
- 1 cup of mushrooms, sliced
- 4 eggs, whisked
- ½ teaspoon of coriander, ground
- Salt and black pepper to the taste
- ½ cup of coconut cream
- ½ teaspoon of turmeric powder
- 4 bacon slices, chopped

Directions:
1. Prepare your Sous-vide in a water bath to a temperature of 140 °F.
2. Vacuum seal all the listed ingredients and lower the pouch in the water bath.
3. Cook for 30 minutes.
4. Serve and enjoy!

Nutrition:
- Calories: 340
- Fat: 23 g
- Protein: 17 g

CHAPTER 6.   LUNCH

18. MIXED VEGETABLES

Preparation Time: 15 minutes

Cooking Time: 3 hours

Servings: 4

Ingredients:

- 1 potato, peeled and diced
- 1 butternut squash, peeled and diced
- 1/2 cauliflower head, diced into florets
- 6 carrots, peeled and diced
- 1 parsnip, peeled and diced
- 1/2 red onion, peeled and diced
- 4 garlic cloves, crushed
- 4 sprigs of fresh rosemary
- 2 tablespoons of olive oil
- Salt and black pepper, to taste
- 2 tablespoons of butter

Directions:

1. Prepare and preheat the sous vide water bath at 185 °F.
2. Add the vegetables and all the ingredients to a zipper-lock bag.
3. Seal the zipper-lock bag using the water immersion method.
4. Place the sealed bag in the sous vide bath and cook for 3 hours.
5. Once done, transfer the vegetables along with the sauce to a plate.
6. Serve.

Nutrition:

- Calories 244
- Fat 13.2 g
- Protein 3.5 g

19. BUTTERY MAPLE CARROTS

Preparation Time: 15 minutes
Cooking Time: 2 hours
Servings: 6
Ingredients:

- 6 baby carrots
- 2 tablespoons of maple syrup
- Salt, to taste
- Black pepper, to taste
- 4 tablespoons of butter, melted

Directions:
1. Prepare and preheat the sous vide water bath at 180 °F.
2. Add the carrots and all the ingredients to a zipper-lock bag.
3. Seal the zipper-lock bag using the water immersion method.
4. Place the sealed bag in the sous vide bath and cook for 2 hours.
5. Once done, transfer the carrots along with the sauce to a plate.
6. Serve.

Nutrition:

- Calories 89
- Fat 7.7 g
- Protein 0.1 g

20. BACON ASPARAGUS

Preparation Time: 15 minutes
Cooking Time: 45 minutes
Servings: 2
Ingredients:

- 1/2 lb. of asparagus, chopped
- Salt, to taste
- Black pepper, to taste
- 2 bacon slices, cooked and chopped
- 2 tablespoons of honey
- 1 teaspoon of lemon juice

Directions:
1. Prepare and preheat the sous vide water bath at 190 °F.
2. Add the asparagus and all the ingredients to a zipper-lock bag.
3. Seal the zipper-lock bag using the water immersion method.
4. Place the sealed bag in the sous vide bath and cook for 45 minutes.
5. Once done, transfer the asparagus to a plate.
6. Serve.

Nutrition:
- Calories: 190
- Fat: 8.1 g
- Protein: 8.6 g

21. BUTTER-GLAZED SWEET POTATOES

Preparation Time: 10 minutes
Cooking Time: 1 hour
Servings: 4
Ingredients:

- 1 lb. of sweet potatoes, peeled and halved
- 2 tablespoons of butter
- 1 tablespoon of olive oil
- 1 tablespoon of fresh thyme, minced
- 2 teaspoons of salt
- 1 teaspoon of black pepper

Directions:

1. Prepare and preheat the sous vide water bath at 190 °F.
2. Add the potatoes and all the ingredients to a zipper-lock bag.
3. Seal the zipper-lock bag using the water immersion method.
4. Place the sealed bag in the sous vide bath and cook for 1 hour.
5. Once done, transfer the potatoes along with the sauce to a plate.
6. Serve.

Nutrition:

- Calories: 198
- Fat: 9.5 g
- Protein: 1.7 g

22. FINGERLING POTATOES WITH ROSEMARY

Preparation Time: 10 minutes
Cooking Time: 2 hours
Servings: 12
Ingredients:

- 2 tablespoons of olive oil
- 4 garlic cloves, peeled
- 1 sprig of fresh rosemary, chopped
- 12 fingerling potatoes, washed
- Salt, to taste
- Black pepper, to taste

Directions:
1. Prepare and preheat the sous vide water bath at 194 °F.
2. Add the potatoes and all the ingredients to a zipper-lock bag.
3. Seal the zipper-lock bag using the water immersion method.
4. Place the sealed bag in the sous vide bath and cook for 2 hours.
5. Once done, transfer the potatoes along with the sauce to a plate.
6. Serve.

Nutrition:

- Calories: 85
- Fat: 2.7 g
- Protein: 1.8 g

23. SESAME EGGPLANT

Preparation Time: 20 minutes
Cooking Time: 3 hours 5 minutes
Servings: 2
Ingredients:

- 1 eggplant, cut into 1/2-inch slices
- 1/4 cup of Worcestershire sauce
- 2 tablespoons of red wine
- 1 tablespoon of soy sauce
- 1 tablespoon of sugar
- 1 teaspoon of sesame oil
- Salt, to taste
- 2 tablespoons of sesame seeds, toasted
- 2 tablespoons of scallions, sliced

Directions:
1. Prepare and preheat the sous vide water bath at 185 °F.
2. Add the sliced eggplant to a zipper-lock bag.
3. Seal the zipper-lock bag using the water immersion method.
4. Place the sealed bag in the sous vide bath and cook for 3 hours.
5. Once done, transfer the eggplant to a plate.
6. Mix the remaining sauce ingredients except sesame seeds in a bowl and pour over the eggplant.
7. Spread the eggplant in a baking tray and broil for 5 minutes.
8. Garnish with sesame seeds.
9. Serve.

Nutrition:
- Calories 200
- Fat 7.2 g
- Protein 4.5 g

24. MAPLE BUTTERNUT SQUASH

Preparation Time: 20 minutes
Cooking Time: 1 hour
Servings: 2
Ingredients:
- 1 butternut squash, peeled, and dice
- 1 tablespoon of maple syrup
- 1 teaspoon of fresh thyme, chopped
- 1/2 teaspoon of garlic powder
- 1 tablespoon of pancetta, chopped
- Salt and black pepper, to taste
- 2 tablespoons of pumpkin seeds, toasted, to garnish

Directions:
1. Prepare and preheat the sous vide water bath at 172 °F.
2. Add the butternut squash and all the ingredients to a zipper-lock bag.
3. Seal the zipper-lock bag using the water immersion method.
4. Place the sealed bag in the sous vide bath and cook for 1 hour.
5. Once done, transfer the squash along with the sauce to a plate.
6. Serve.

Nutrition:
- Calories: 160
- Fat: 8.1 g
- Protein: 6.5 g

25. ZUCCHINI MEDALLIONS

Preparation Time: 15 minutes
Cooking Time: 30 minutes
Servings: 2
Ingredients:

- 2 zucchinis, sliced
- 2 tablespoons of butter
- Salt and black pepper, to taste

Directions:

1. Prepare and preheat the sous vide water bath at 185 °F.
2. Add the zucchini and all the ingredients to a zipper-lock bag.
3. Seal the zipper-lock bag using the water immersion method.
4. Place the sealed bag in the sous vide bath and cook for 30 minutes.
5. Once done, transfer the zucchini along with the sauce to a plate.
6. Serve.

Nutrition:

- Calories: 133
- Fat: 11.9 g
- Protein: 2.5 g

26. GARLICKY RATATOUILLE

Preparation Time: 15 minutes

Cooking Time: 2 hours

Servings: 4

Ingredients:

- 2 teaspoons of red pepper flakes
- 1 yellow bell pepper, cored and sliced
- 1 eggplant, sliced
- 1 red bell pepper, cored and sliced
- 3 zucchinis, sliced
- 1 onion, peeled and sliced
- 1/2 cup of tomato puree
- Salt, to taste
- 10 garlic cloves, peeled and minced
- 5 tablespoons of avocado oil
- 5 sprigs fresh basil, chopped

Directions:

1. Prepare and preheat the sous vide water bath at 185 °F.
2. Add the veggies and all the ingredients to a zipper-lock bag.
3. Seal the zipper-lock bag using the water immersion method.
4. Place the sealed bag in the sous vide bath and cook for 2 hours.
5. Once done, transfer the veggies along with the sauce to a plate.
6. Serve.

Nutrition:

- Calories: 264
- Fat: 18.6 g
- Protein: 5.3 g

27. BACON-BRUSSELS SPROUTS

Preparation Time: 15 minutes

Cooking Time: 1 hour

Servings: 2

Ingredients:

- 4 slices of bacon, cooked
- 2 garlic cloves
- 1/2 lb. of Brussels sprouts

Directions:

1. Prepare and preheat the sous vide water bath at 172 °F.
2. Add the brussels sprouts and all the ingredients to a zipper-lock bag.
3. Seal the zipper-lock bag using the water immersion method.
4. Place the sealed bag in the sous vide bath and cook for 1 hour.
5. Once done, transfer the Brussels sprout mixture to a plate.
6. Serve.

Nutrition:

- Calories: 259
- Fat: 16.3 g
- Protein: 18.1 g

28. CIDER DIPPED FENNEL

Preparation Time: 15 minutes

Cooking Time: 1 hour

Servings: 2

Ingredients:

- 1/2 lb. of fennel bulbs, chopped
- Salt, to taste
- 2 tablespoons of apple cider vinegar
- Black pepper, to taste

Directions:

1. Prepare and preheat the sous vide water bath at 190 °F.
2. Add the fennel and all the ingredients to a zipper-lock bag.
3. Seal the zipper-lock bag using the water immersion method.
4. Place the sealed bag in the sous vide bath and cook for 1 hour.
5. Once done, transfer the fennel along with the sauce to a plate.
6. Serve.

Nutrition:

- Calories: 67
- Fat: 0.4 g
- Protein: 2.2 g

29. GARLIC BROCCOLI

Preparation Time: 15 minutes

Cooking Time: 20 minutes

Servings: 2

Ingredients:

- 1 broccoli head, cut into florets
- 3 garlic cloves, peeled
- 1/4 cup of olive oil
- 1 teaspoon of dried rosemary
- Salt, to taste
- Black pepper, to taste

Directions:

1. Prepare and preheat the sous vide water bath at 194 °F.
2. Add the broccoli and all the ingredients to a zipper-lock bag.
3. Seal the zipper-lock bag using the water immersion method.
4. Place the sealed bag in the sous vide bath and cook for 20 minutes.
5. Once done, transfer the broccoli along with the sauce to a plate.
6. Serve.

Nutrition:

- Calories: 240
- Fat: 25.5 g
- Protein: 1.6 g

30. LEMON-BUTTER SHRIMP

Preparation Time: 9 minutes

Cooking Time: 30 minutes

Serving: 8

Ingredients:

- 2 pounds of large shrimp, peeled, deveined
- 16 strips (½ inch each) of lemon zest
- 4 ounces of chilled butter, cut into 8 slices
- 1 teaspoon of creole seasoning or to taste + extra to serve
- 6 sprigs of fresh thyme

Directions:

1. Follow the instructions given in the manual and fill the sous vide water oven. Preheat it to 135 °F.
2. Place the shrimps in a bowl. Sprinkle creole seasoning on top and toss well.
3. Transfer into a large Ziploc bag or vacuum-seal pouch. Spread the shrimp in a single layer. Use 2 pouches, if required.
4. Scatter the lemon zest, butter, and thyme all over the shrimp. Vacuum seal the pouch.
5. Submerge the pouch in a water bath and adjust the timer for 30 minutes.
6. When the timer goes off, remove the pouch from the water bath.
7. Transfer the shrimp onto a serving platter. Sprinkle some more creole seasoning on top and serve.

Nutrition:

- Calories: 534
- Fat: 20 g
- Protein: 13 g

CHAPTER 7. DINNER RECIPES

31. TENDER PORK CHOPS

Preparation Time: 5 minutes
Cooking Time: 2 hours
Serving: 2
Ingredients:
- 2 pork chops
- 1 tablespoon of canola oil
- 1 tablespoon of butter
- 4 garlic cloves
- 1 teaspoon of Rosemary
- 1 teaspoon of Thyme
- ¼ tsp of Pepper
- ¼ tsp of Salt

Directions:
1. Preheat water oven to 140 °F / 60 °C.
2. Season the pork with pepper and salt. Place pork chops into the zip-lock bag.
3. Remove all the air from the bag before sealing. Place the bag into the hot water bath and cook for 2 hours.
4. Remove pork from bag and pat dry with a paper towel.
5. Heat oil and butter in a pan over high heat with rosemary, thyme, and garlic.
6. Place pork chops in a pan-sear until lightly brown, about 1 minute on each side.
7. Serve and enjoy.

Nutrition:
- Calories: 378
- Fat: 32 g
- Protein: 18 g

32. PORK CHOPS WITH MUSHROOMS

Preparation Time: 10 minutes
Cooking Time: 2 hours 10 minutes
Serving: 4
Ingredients:
- 4 pork chops, boneless
- 4 tablespoons of butter
- 2 garlic cloves, minced
- 1 tablespoon of flour
- 1 cup of chicken broth
- 8 oz. of Cremini mushrooms, sliced
- 1 large shallot, sliced
- Pepper
- Salt

Directions:
1. Preheat water oven to 140 °F / 60 °C.
2. Place the chops into a zip-lock bag. Place the bag into a water bath and cook for 2 hours.
3. Remove chops from bag and pat dry with a paper towel.
4. Season the chop with salt and pepper.
5. Heat 2 tablespoons of butter in a pan. Sear the chops on both sides.
6. Add the remaining 2 tablespoons of butter to a pan. Add sliced mushrooms to the pan and cook for 4-5 minutes, occasionally stirring.
7. Add the shallots cook for 2 minutes until tender, add garlic, stir for 1 minute constantly, and add flour.
8. Stir well until mixture is evenly coated over mushrooms, add chicken broth stir for 1 minute.
9. Season with salt and pepper.
10. Serve and enjoy.

Nutrition:
- Calories: 392
- Fat: 31.8 g
- Protein: 21 g

33. PORK TENDERLOIN

Preparation Time: 10 minutes

Cooking Time: 2 hours 10 minutes

Serving: 2

Ingredients:

- 16 oz. of pork tenderloin
- 1 tablespoon of olive oil
- 1 tablespoon of butter
- 2 small shallots, sliced
- 2 garlic cloves
- 8 sprigs of fresh herbs
- Black pepper
- Kosher salt

Directions:

1. Preheat a water oven to 150 °F / 66 °C.
2. Season the pork with salt and pepper.
3. Place the pork into a zip-lock bag. Remove all the air from the bag before sealing.
4. Place the bag into the hot water bath and Cook for 2 hours.
5. Remove the pork from the zip-lock bag and pat dry with a paper towel.
6. Heat olive oil in a pan over medium heat. Add pork and cook for 2 minutes until lightly browned.
7. Add the butter with fresh herbs, shallots, and garlic. Cook for 1 minute.
8. Serve and enjoy.

Nutrition:

- Calories: 440
- Fat: 20.7 g
- Protein: 59.6 g

34. HERB RUB PORK CHOPS

Preparation Time: 10 minutes
Cooking Time: 2 hours 10 minutes
Serving: 4
Ingredients:

- 4 pork chops, bone-in
- 1/4 cup of olive oil
- 1 teaspoon of black pepper
- 1 tablespoon of balsamic vinegar
- 1 lemon zest
- 2 garlic cloves, minced
- 6 thyme sprigs, remove stems
- 1/4 cup of chives
- 1/4 cup of rosemary
- 10 basil leaves
- 1/4 cup of parsley
- 1/2 teaspoon of salt

Directions:

1. Fill and preheat sous vide water oven to 140 °F/ 60 °C.
2. Add herbs to the food processor and process until chopped.
3. Add garlic, olive oil, pepper, salt, vinegar, and lemon zest and blend until a smooth paste is formed.
4. Rub herb mixture over pork chops. Place pork chops into the zip-lock bag and remove all the air from the bag before sealing.
5. Place the bag into the hot water bath and cook for 2 hours.
6. Remove pork chops from the water bath and boil for 3-4 minutes.
7. Serve and enjoy.

Nutrition:

- Calories: 383
- Fat: 33.1 g
- Protein: 18.6 g

35. BONE-IN PORK CHOP

Preparation Time: 5 minutes
Cooking Time: 2 hours 10 minutes
Serving: 2
Ingredients:
- 2 pork chops, bone-in
- 1 teaspoon of olive oil
- 1/8 teaspoon of tarragon
- 1/8 teaspoon of thyme
- Black pepper
- Salt

Directions:
1. Fill and preheat the sous vide water oven to 145 °F/ 62 °C.
2. Season pork chops with pepper and salt.
3. Rub the tarragon, olive oil, and thyme over pork chops.
4. Place pork chops into the zip-lock bag and remove all the air from the bag before sealing.
5. Place the bag into the hot water bath and cook for 2 hours.
6. Remove pork chops from bag and sear until lightly brown.
7. Serve and enjoy.

Nutrition:
- Calories: 276
- Fat: 22.2 g
- Protein: 18 g

36. PORK LOIN

Preparation Time: 5 minutes
Cooking Time: 4 hours
Serving: 4
Ingredients:

- 2 lbs. of pork loin roast
- 2 tablespoon of sweet and sour sauce
- 1 teaspoon of black pepper
- 1 teaspoon of garlic powder
- 1/2 teaspoon of chipotle powder
- 1 teaspoon of salt

Directions:

1. Fill and preheat the sous vide water oven to 153 °F/ 67 °C.
2. In a small bowl, mix the chipotle powder, garlic powder, black pepper, and salt.
3. Rub spice mixture over the pork loin roast.
4. Place pork into the zip-lock bag and remove all the air from the bag before sealing.
5. Place the bag into the hot water bath and cook for 4 hours.
6. Remove pork from bag and coat outside with sweet and sour sauce.
7. Broil pork for 5 minutes until lightly brown.
8. Serve and enjoy.

Nutrition:

- Calories: 487
- Fat: 21.9 g
- Protein: 65.1 g

37. LEMON PORK CHOPS

Preparation Time: 5 minutes
Cooking Time: 6 hours
Serving: 4
Ingredients:

- 4 pork chops, bone-in
- 1 lemon, sliced
- 4 fresh thyme sprigs, chopped
- 1 tablespoon of olive oil
- Pepper
- Salt

Directions:

1. Fill and preheat sous vide water oven to 138 °F/ 59 °C.
2. Season pork chops with pepper and salt.
3. Place the pork chops into the zip-lock bag with thyme and lemon slices. Drizzle with olive oil.
4. Remove all air from the bag before sealing.
5. Place the bag into the hot water bath and cook for 6 hours.
6. Remove pork chops from the bag and pat dry with a paper towel.
7. Using a kitchen torch, sear the pork chops until caramelizing.
8. Serve and enjoy.

Nutrition:

- Calories: 286
- Fat: 23.4 g
- Protein: 18 g

38. BBQ PORK RIBS

Preparation Time: 5 minutes

Cooking Time: 18 hours

Serving: 2

Ingredients:

- 1 rack of back ribs, cut into rib portions
- 2 tablespoons of Worcestershire sauce
- 1/3 cup of brown sugar
- 1 1/2 cups of BBQ sauce

Directions:

1. Fill and preheat sous vide water oven to 160 °F/ 75 °C.
2. Whisk the brown sugar in 1 cup of BBQ sauce and Worcestershire sauce.
3. Place the ribs into the large mixing bowl, then pour marinade over the ribs and toss well.
4. Place the ribs into the zip-lock bag and remove all the air from the bag before sealing.
5. Place the bag into the hot water bath and cook for 18 hours.
6. Remove ribs from bag and place on a baking tray.
7. Brush ribs with remaining BBQ sauce and broil for 5 minutes.
8. Serve and enjoy.

Nutrition:

- Calories: 663
- Fat: 19 g
- Protein: 10 g

39. FIVE-SPICE PORK

Preparation Time: 5 minutes

Cooking Time: 48 hours

Serving: 4

Ingredients:

- 1 lb. of pork belly
- 1 bacon slice
- 1 teaspoon of Chinese 5 spice powder
- Black pepper
- Salt

Directions:

1. Fill and preheat sous vide water oven to 140 °F/ 60 °C.
2. Add the pork belly into the zip-lock bag with bacon slice and seasonings.
3. Remove all the air from the bag before sealing.
4. Place the bag into the hot water bath and cook for 48 hours.
5. Remove pork from bag and broil until crisp.
6. Serve and enjoy.

Nutrition:

- Calories: 549
- Fat: 32 g
- Protein: 54 g

40. BBQ BABY BACK RIBS

Preparation Time: 5 minutes

Cooking Time: 24 hours

Serving: 2

Ingredients:

- 1 rack of baby back pork ribs
- 6 tablespoons of Chipotle BBQ sauce
- Pepper
- Salt

Directions:

1. Fill and preheat the sous vide water oven to 143 °F/ 61 °C.
2. Cut the rib rack in half and season with pepper and salt.
3. Brush the BBQ sauce over the pork ribs.
4. Place ribs into the zip-lock bag and remove all the air from the bag before sealing.
5. Place the bag into the hot water bath and cook for 24 hours.
6. Remove ribs from bag and grill for 1 minute.
7. Serve and enjoy.

Nutrition:

- Calories: 850
- Fat: 48 g
- Protein: 45 g

41. PORK CARNITAS

Preparation Time: 10 minutes
Cooking Time: 20 hours 10 minutes
Serving: 12
Ingredients:

- 6 lb. of pork shoulder
- 2 tablespoons of anise
- 2 bay leaves
- 2 cinnamon sticks
- 3 tablespoons of garlic, minced
- 4 bacon slices
- 1/3 cup of brown sugar
- 2 orange juices
- 1 onion, chopped
- 1 tablespoon of sea salt

Directions:

1. Fill and preheat sous vide water oven to 175 °F/ 79 °C.
2. In a small bowl, mix the anise, sugar, salt, garlic, and orange juice.
3. Place pork into the zip-lock bag then pour orange juice mixture over pork.
4. Add cinnamon, bay leaves, bacon, and onions into the bag.
5. Seal bag and place into the hot water bath and cook for 20 hours.
6. Heat a large pan over medium-high heat.
7. Remove pork from bag and place on pan and shred using a fork.
8. Cook the shredded pork until crispy.
9. Serve and enjoy.

Nutrition:

- Calories: 729
- Fat: 51 g
- Protein: 55 g

42. PULLED PORK

Preparation Time: 10 minutes

Cooking Time: 18 hours 35 minutes

Serving: 4

Ingredients:

- 2 lb. of pork shoulder, boneless
- 1/2 cup of taco seasoning
- 1/4 cup of cilantro, chopped

Directions:

1. Fill and preheat the sous vide water oven to 165 °F/ 73 °C.
2. Season the pork with half of the taco seasoning.
3. Place the pork into the zip-lock bag and remove all the air from the bag before sealing.
4. Place the bag into the hot water bath and cook for 18 hours.
5. Remove pork from bag and pat dry with a paper towel.
6. Season pork with remaining taco seasoning.
7. Place the pork in preheated 350 °F/ 176 °C oven and cook for 30 minutes.
8. Remove pork from the oven and, using a fork, shred the pork.
9. Garnish with cilantro and serve.

Nutrition:

- Calories: 733
- Fat: 48 g
- Protein: 53 g

43. SIMPLE SLICED PORK BELLY

Preparation Time: 10 minutes

Cooking Time: 3 hours 10 minutes

Serving: 2

Ingredients:

- 4 oz. of pork belly, sliced
- 3 bay leaves
- 1 tablespoon of garlic salt
- 1 tablespoon of whole black peppercorns
- 1 1/2 tablespoon of olive oil

Directions:

1. Fill and preheat the sous vide water oven to 145 °F/ 62 °C.
2. Add the sliced pork belly, bay leaves, garlic salt, peppercorns, and 1 tablespoon of olive oil into the large zip-lock bag.
3. Remove all the air from the bag before sealing.
4. Place the bag into the hot water bath and cook for 3 hours.
5. Heat the remaining oil in a pan over medium heat.
6. Remove pork from bag and sear in hot oil for 2 minutes on each side.
7. Serve and enjoy.

Nutrition:

- Calories: 374
- Fat: 25 g
- Protein: 27 g

44. PERFECT PORK CHOP

Preparation Time: 5 minutes

Cooking Time: 50 minutes

Serving: 2

Ingredients:

- 20 oz. of pork rib chop, bone-in
- 2 tablespoon of butter
- Black pepper
- Salt

Directions:

1. Fill and preheat the sous vide water oven to 140 °F/ 60 °C.
2. Season the pork chops with pepper and salt.
3. Place the pork chops into the zip-lock bag and remove all the air from the bag before sealing.
4. Place the bag into the hot water bath and cook for 45 minutes.
5. Heat the butter into the pan over medium heat.
6. Remove the pork chop from the bag and pat dry with a paper towel.
7. Sear pork chops in hot butter until lightly brown from both sides.
8. Serve and enjoy.

Nutrition:

- Calories: 731
- Fat: 48 g
- Protein: 69 g

45. SWEET AND SPICY PORK RIBS

Preparation Time: 5 minutes

Cooking Time: 20 hours 10 minutes

Serving: 6

Ingredients:

- 2 full racks of baby back pork ribs, cut in half
- 1/2 cup of jerk seasoning mix

Directions:

1. Fill and preheat the sous vide water oven to 145 °F/ 62 °C.
2. Season the pork rib rack with half-jerk seasoning and place it in a large zip-lock bag.
3. Remove all the air from the bag before sealing.
4. Place the bag into the hot water bath and cook for 20 hours.
5. Remove meat from bag and rub with remaining seasoning and place on a baking tray.
6. Broil for 5 minutes. Slice and serve.

Nutrition:

- Calories: 880
- Fat: 56 g
- Protein: 56 g

46. ROSEMARY GARLIC LAMB CHOPS

Preparation Time: 5 minutes

Cooking Time: 2 hours 30 minutes

Serving: 4

Ingredients:

- 4 lamb chops
- 1 tablespoon of butter
- 1 teaspoon of fresh thyme
- 1 teaspoon of fresh rosemary
- 2 garlic cloves
- Pepper
- Salt

Directions:

1. Fill and preheat sous vide water oven to 140 °F/ 60 °C.
2. Season the lamb chops with pepper and salt.
3. Sprinkle the lamb chops with garlic, thyme, and rosemary.
4. Add butter to the zip-lock bag, then place lamb chops into the bag.
5. Remove all the air from the bag before sealing.
6. Place bag in a hot water bath and cook for 2 1/2 hours.
7. Once it is done, sear it on high heat until lightly brown.
8. Serve and enjoy.

Nutrition:

- Calories: 349
- Fat: 29 g
- Protein: 19.2 g

CHAPTER 8.   RED MEATS

47.   SIMPLE RACK OF LAMB

Preparation Time: 5 minutes

Cooking Time: 2 hours

Serving: 4

Ingredients:

- 2 lbs. of rack of lamb
- 2 tablespoons of butter
- 2 tablespoons of canola oil
- Black pepper
- Salt

Directions:

1. Fill and preheat sous vide water oven to 140 °F/ 60 °C.
2. Season the lamb with pepper and salt and place it in a large zip-lock bag.
3. Remove all air from the bag before sealing.
4. Place bag in a hot water bath and cook for 2 hours.
5. Remove lamb from the bag and pat dry with paper towels.
6. Heat the canola oil in a pan over medium heat.
7. Spread the butter over lamb and sear lamb in hot oil until lightly brown.
8. Serve and enjoy.

Nutrition:

- Calories: 494
- Fat: 32.8 g
- Protein: 46.2 g

48. HERB GARLIC LAMB CHOPS

Preparation Time: 10 minutes

Cooking Time: 2 hours

Serving: 4

Ingredients:

- 4 lamb chops, bone-in
- 2 tablespoons of butter
- 8 black peppercorns
- 1 teaspoon of fresh oregano
- 1 tablespoon of fresh parsley
- 1 bay leaf
- 4 fresh thyme sprigs
- 2 teaspoon of garlic, sliced
- Sea salt

Directions:

1. Fill and preheat the sous vide water oven to 132 °F/ 56 °C.
2. Add the lamb, butter, peppercorns, herbs, and garlic into the large zip-lock bag and remove all the air from the bag before sealing.
3. Place the bag into the hot water bath and cook for 2 hours.
4. Remove lamb chops from bag and pat dry with paper towels.
5. Heat pan over high heat and sear lamb chops for 30 seconds on each side.
6. Serve and enjoy.

Nutritions:

- Calories: 663
- Fat: 29.8 g
- Protein: 92.1 g

49. BONELESS STRIP STEAK

Preparation Time: 31 minutes
Cooking Time: 2 hours 30 minutes
Serving: 2
Ingredients:
- 1 14–16-ounces of boneless strip steak, 1½–2 inches thick
- ¼ teaspoon of garlic powder
- ¼ teaspoon of onion powder
- 1 teaspoon of kosher salt, plus more
- ¼ teaspoon of freshly ground black pepper, plus more
- 3 sprigs of rosemary
- 3 sprigs of thyme
- 1 teaspoon of grapeseed or other neutral oil

Directions:
1. Preheat your sous vide to 130°F or 54.5°C for a medium-rare steak. Change the temperature to 5 °F in either direction to adjust wellness.
2. Mix the garlic powder, onion powder, 1 teaspoon of salt, ¼ teaspoon of pepper in a bowl.
3. Rub the mixture all over all 4 sides of the steak. Smack the sprigs of herbs against a cutting board.
4. Place the steak in the bag you're going to use to sous vide, along with the sprigs of herbs, and seal the bag.
5. Place the bag in your preheated water. Set timer for 2 hours and 30 minutes.
6. When the steak is ready, allow it to rest for 15 minutes.
7. Take the steak out of the bag and let it rest for a few more minutes.
8. While it's resting, season it with salt and pepper to taste.
9. Heat a skittle (ideally cast iron) on high heat. When it gets really hot, pour in the oil and put it in the steak. Let the steak sear for 1 to 2 minutes total, flipping it on all four sides. The steak should form a very nice crust on all sides.
10. Serve immediately.

Nutrition:
- Calories: 541
- Fat: 36 g
- Protein: 57 g

50. KOREAN KALBI SHORT RIBS

Preparation Time: 19 minutes
Cooking Time: 2 hours 30 minutes
Serving: 4
Ingredients:
- 16 Korean Style crosscut beef short ribs

Marinade:
- 2 tablespoons of sesame oil
- 2 tablespoons of brown sugar
- 1 ½ teaspoon of chili flakes
- 1 tablespoon of chopped garlic
- ½ cup of soy sauce
- ¼ cup of chopped green onions
- ¼ cup of orange juice

Directions:
1. Heat a pan on medium-high heat and add in the sesame oil and garlic. Allow the garlic to cook for 2 minutes, then take the pan off the heat. Add the rest of the marinade ingredients to the pan while it's still warm, and stir the mixture until well combined.
2. Place the ribs in a baking dish and pour in the marinade. Place the dish in the refrigerator, covered for 1 hr. Turn the meat every 15 min.
3. Preheat your sous vide to 138 °F or 59 °C.
4. Save the marinade for later.
5. Place the steak in the bag you're going to use to sous. Seal the bag.
6. Place the bag in your preheated water and set the timer for 3 hours.
7. While the meat is cooking, put the marinade in a pot and allow it to come to a boil. Allow the sauce to cook for 15 to 20 minutes until it starts to reduce a little.
8. When the ribs are almost done, preheat your broiler.
9. When the steaks are cooked, use a brush to coat them with the marinade.
10. Place the ribs on an aluminum foil-rimmed baking sheet or pan.
11. Put the baking sheet under the broiler and allow the meat to cook for 1 to 2 minutes per side. You just want the sauce to caramelize.
12. Serve the ribs immediately.

Nutrition:
- Calories: 508
- Fat: 30 g
- Protein: 56 g

51. HANGER STEAK

Preparation Time: 6 minutes
Cooking Time: 4 hours
Serving: 4
Ingredients:

- 4 (8 oz.) pieces of hanger steak
- Kosher or truffle salt
- Freshly ground black pepper
- 12 sprigs thyme
- 2 garlic cloves
- 2 shallots, peeled and thinly sliced
- 2 tablespoons of high-smoke point oil

Directions:

1. Preheat your sous vide to 130 °F or 54.5 °C for a medium-rare steak. Change the temperature to 10 °F in either direction to adjust wellness.
2. Season the steak with salt and pepper to taste.
3. Place the steak in the bag you're going to use to sous-vide along with the sprigs of thyme, garlic, and shallots. Divide the herbs, garlic, and shallots among the 4 steaks, place thyme sprigs, shallots slices on both sides, and seal the bag.
4. Place the bag in your preheated water and set the timer for 4 hours.
5. When the steak is ready, allow it to rest for a few minutes.
6. While it's resting, heat a skittle (ideally cast iron) on high heat. When it gets really hot, pour in the oil and put it in the steak. Let the steak sear for 1 minute per side. It should form a nice crust on both sides.
7. Serve immediately.

Nutrition:

- Calories: 577
- Fat: 32 g
- Protein: 50 g

52. SPICE-RUBBED SHORT RIBS

Preparation Time: 11 minutes
Cooking Time: 48 hours
Serving: 6
Ingredients:
- 3 lbs. of beef short ribs
- 1 tablespoon of ground cumin
- 1 tablespoon of ancho chili powder
- 1/4 teaspoon of ground cloves
- 1 teaspoon of Kosher salt
- 1 teaspoon of freshly ground black pepper

Directions:
1. Preheat your sous vide to 140 °F or 60 °C.
2. Combine the spices in a bowl. Coat the beef ribs with the spice rub.
3. Place the steak in the bag or bags you're going to use to sous vide and seal the bag or bags.
4. Place the bag in your preheated water and set the timer for 48 hours.
5. When the ribs are almost ready, preheat your broiler
6. Place the cooked ribs on an aluminum foil-rimmed baking sheet or pan. Broil for about 5 minutes until you see the edges char.
7. Serve immediately.

Nutrition:
- Calories: 428
- Fat: 26.1 g
- Protein: 67 g

53. BEEF SHOGAYAKI

Preparation Time: 11 minutes

Cooking Time: 12 hours

Serving: 3

Ingredients:

- 18 oz. Beef Stew Meat
- 3 tablespoons of Soy Sauce
- 3 tablespoons of Mirin
- 3 tablespoons of Water
- 1 Thumb-Sized Piece Ginger grated
- 1 tablespoon of high-smoke point oil

Directions:

1. Preheat your sous vide to 140 °F or 60 °C.
2. Mix the soy, water, ginger, and mirin in a bowl. Add the beef, and toss it in the mixture to coat.
3. Place the beef in the bag you're going to use to sous-vide along with the sauce and seal the bag.
4. Place the bag in your preheated water and set the timer for 12 hours.
5. When the beef is ready, heat a skittle (ideally cast iron) on high heat.
6. When it gets really hot, pour in the oil and put in the beef. Let the steak sear for 1 minute, flipping halfway through. The steak should form a nice crust on both sides.

Nutrition:

- Calories: 498
- Fat: 41.1 g
- Protein: 67 g

54. BEEF MEATBALLS

Preparation Time: 11 minutes
Cooking Time: 60 minutes
Serving: 3
Ingredients:
- 11 oz. of Ground Beef
- 1 Egg
- 4 cloves of garlic, minced
- 1 Piece of Shallot, minced
- 1/4 cup of Bread Crumbs
- 1/4 teaspoon of Granulated Ginger
- 1/4 teaspoon of Garlic Powder
- 1/4 teaspoon of Cumin Powder
- 1/4 teaspoon of Black Pepper Powder
- 1/2 teaspoon of Paprika Powder
- 2 tablespoons of Yogurt
- 1 teaspoon of Salt
- 1 teaspoon of Liquid Smoke
- 1 tablespoon of high-smoke point oil

Directions:
1. Preheat your sous vide to 140 °F or 60 °C.
2. Mix all the ingredients in a bowl.
3. Use your hands to make the mixture into 8 equal size balls.
4. Put the balls on a baking sheet and cover with plastic wrap or aluminum foil. Place the baking sheet in the refrigerator for 10 minutes.
5. Place the beef in the bag you're going to use to sous vide and seal the bag.
6. Place the bag in your preheated water and set the timer for 1 hour.
7. When the meatballs are ready, heat a skittle (ideally cast iron) on high heat.
8. When it gets really hot, pour in the oil and put in the beef. Let the meatballs sear for 1 minute, flipping halfway through. The meatballs should brown on both sides.

Nutrition:
- Calories: 508
- Fat: 46.1 g
- Protein: 58 g

55. ROAST BEEF

Preparation Time: 16 minutes

Cooking Time: 24 hours

Serving: 8

Ingredients:

- 3 1/2 lb. of beef roast
- 2 cloves of garlic minced
- 1 tablespoon of rosemary minced
- 1/2 tablespoon of Worcestershire sauce
- 1 teaspoon of smoked paprika
- 1/2 teaspoon of mustard powder
- 1/2 teaspoon of onion powder
- 2 1/2 teaspoon of salt
- 1/2 teaspoon of pepper

Directions:

1. Preheat your sous vide to 136 °F or 58 °C.
2. Combine all the ingredients, except for the beef and Worcestershire sauce, in a bowl.
3. Rub the Worcestershire sauce all over the beef, then coat the beef with the spice mixture.
4. Place the beef in the bag you're going to use to sous vide and seal the bag.
5. Place the bag in your preheated water and set the timer for 24 hours.
6. When the beef is almost ready, preheat your oven to 350 °F.
7. Place the cooked roast on a broiler pan.
8. Place the roast in the oven and allow it to cook for 15 minutes.

Nutrition:

- Calories: 498
- Fat: 46.1 g
- Protein: 61 g

56. TUSCAN RIB EYE STEAK

Preparation Time: 11 minutes
Cooking Time: 30 minutes
Serving: 4
Ingredients:

- 4 tablespoons of extra virgin olive oil
- 2 tablespoons of finely chopped garlic
- 1 tablespoon of ground black pepper
- 1 tablespoon of ground fennel
- 2 tablespoons of chopped anchovies
- 2 tablespoons of chopped parsley
- 1 tablespoon of chopped rosemary
- 4, 10 to 12 oz. natural boneless rib-eye steaks
- 2 tablespoons of olive oil
- kosher salt

Directions:

1. Preheat your sous vide to 168 °F or 75.5 °C.
2. Heat a skillet on medium heat and add in the olive oil and garlic. Allow the garlic to cook until it browns, about 4 min. Then put in the anchovies, rosemary, fennel, parsley, and black pepper. Take the skillet off the heat.
3. Season the rib eyes with a little kosher salt. Coat both sides of the steaks with the rosemary mixture.
4. Rub the Worcestershire sauce all over the beef, then coat the beef with the spice mixture.
5. Place each steak in its own bag and seal the bags.
6. Place the bag in your preheated water and set the timer for 30 min.
7. When the steaks are ready, heat a skittle (ideally cast iron) on high heat and get the skillet really hot. Place a little oil in the skillet
8. Place the cooked steaks in the skillet. Sear for about 1 min per side.
9. Serve the steaks immediately.

Nutrition:

- Calories: 488
- Fat: 29.1 g
- Protein: 60 g

57. BURGERS

Preparation Time: 6 minutes
Cooking Time: 60 minutes
Serving: 2
Ingredients:

- 10 oz. of freshly ground beef
- 2 hamburger buns
- 2 slices of American cheese
- Salt
- Pepper
- Condiments and toppings of choice

Directions:

1. Preheat your sous vide to 137 °F or 58.3 °C
2. Use your hands to form the burgers into 2 equal-sized 1 inch thick patties.
3. Place the patties in the bag you're going to use to sous vide and seal the bag.
4. Place the bag in your preheated water and set the timer for 1 hour.
5. When the patties are ready, heat a skittle (ideally cast iron) on high heat.
6. When it gets really hot, put in the patties. Let the patties sear for 1 minute, flipping halfway through. When you flip the burgers, top with cheese slices, so the cheese melts.
7. Serve on buns with the condiments of your choice.

Nutrition:

- Calories: 578
- Fat: 39 g
- Protein: 52 g

58. SMOKED BRISKET

Preparation Time: 2 hours 15 minutes
Cooking Time: 38 hours
Serving: 10
Ingredients:

- 2 oz. of coarsely ground black peppercorns
- 2 1/4 oz. of kosher salt
- 1/4 oz. of pink salt
- 1, 5 lb. of flat-cut or point-cut brisket
- 1/4 teaspoon of liquid smoke

Directions:

1. Mix the different salts and pepper in a bowl. Coat the brisket with about 2/3 of the mixture. Then cut the brisket in half crosswise.
2. Place the 2 briskets in 2 bags, put in 4 drops of liquid smoke in each bag, and seal the bags.
3. Allow the bags to marinate in your refrigerator for 2 to 3 hours.
4. Preheat your sous vide to 155 °F or 68 °C.
5. Place the bag in your preheated water and set the timer for 36 hours.
6. When the brisket is almost ready, move one of your oven racks to the lower-middle position. Preheat your oven to 300 °F.
7. Use a paper towel to pat the cooked brisket dry. Coat the brisket with the remaining seasoning mixture.
8. Put a wire rack on a baking sheet and place the brisket on top of it with the fat side up. Place the brisket in the oven for about 2 hours. The brisket is done when a dark bark forms on the outside
9. Place the brisket on a cutting board and use aluminum foil to tent it. Allow the brisket to rest for 30 min. You want the internal temperature to be between 145F and 165F.
10. Cut the brisket against the grain into desired size pieces and serve.

Nutrition:

- Calories: 538
- Fat: 33 g
- Protein: 50 g

59. SPICE-RUBBED BBQ BABY BACK RIBS

Preparation Time: 16 minutes
Cooking Time: 24 hours 10 minutes
Serving: 8
Ingredients:

- 2 2½-pound of racks baby back ribs, cut in half crosswise
- 1 cup of BBQ of sauce

Rub:

- 2 tablespoons of kosher salt
- 2 tablespoons of smoked paprika
- 2 tablespoons of light brown sugar
- 1 tablespoon of ground cumin
- 1 tablespoon of ground cayenne
- 1 tablespoon of ground coriander

Directions:

1. Preheat your sous vide to 155 °F or 68.3 °C.
2. Place the rub ingredients in a bowl and use a whisk to mix them.
3. Coat the ribs with rub.
4. Place the ribs in the bags you're going to use to sous vide and seal the bags.
5. Place the bags in your preheated water and set the timer for 24 hours.
6. When the ribs are almost ready, preheat a grill on medium-high heat.
7. Baste the ribs with BBQ sauce and place them on the grill. Continue to baste the ribs with BBQ sauce as they cook. Cook for 6 to 8 minutes, flipping frequently. The ribs are done when they start to char.
8. Serve the ribs immediately.

Nutrition:

- Calories: 508
- Fat: 30 g
- Protein: 51 g

CHAPTER 9. VEGETABLE RECIPES

60. SNOW PEAS WITH MINT

Preparation Time: 10 minutes

Cooking Time: 15 minutes

Servings: 2

Ingredients:

- 1 tablespoon of Butter
- ½ cup of Snow Peas
- 1 tablespoon of Mint Leaves, chopped
- A pinch of Salt
- Sugar to taste

Directions:

1. Make a water bath, place a Sous Vide cooker in it, and set it at 183 °F.
2. Place all the ingredients in a vacuum-sealable bag.
3. Release air by the water displacement method, seal the bag and submerge in the water bath.
4. Set the timer for 15 minutes.
5. Once the timer has stopped, remove and unseal the bag.
6. Transfer the ingredients to a serving plate. Serve as a condiment.

Nutrition:

- Calories: 117
- Fat: 0.6 g
- Protein: 8 g

61. HERBED ASPARAGUS MIX

Preparation Time: 15 minutes

Cooking Time: 12 minutes

Servings: 3

Ingredients:

- 1 ½ lb. of medium Asparagus
- 5 tablespoons of Butter
- 2 tablespoons of Lemon Juice
- ½ teaspoon of Lemon Zest
- 1 tablespoon of + tablespoon of Fresh Dill, chopped
- 1 tablespoon of + 1 tablespoon of Tarragon, chopped

Directions:

1. Make a water bath, place the Sous Vide cooker in it, and set it to 183 °F. Cut off and discard the tight bottoms of the asparagus. Place the asparagus in a vacuum-sealable bag.
2. Release air by the water displacement method, seal and submerge the bag in the water bath, and set the timer for 10 minutes.
3. Once the timer has stopped, remove the bag and unseal it. Place a skillet over low heat, add the butter and steamed asparagus. Season with salt and pepper and toss continually. Add lemon juice and zest and cook for 2 minutes.
4. Turn heat off and add parsley, 1 tablespoon of dill, and 1 tablespoon of tarragon. Toss evenly. Garnish with remaining dill and tarragon. Serve warm as a side dish.

Nutrition:

- Calories: 190
- Fat: 0.1 g
- Protein: 2.2 g

62. BALSAMIC BRAISED CABBAGE

Preparation Time: 15 minutes

Cooking Time: 1 hour 30 minutes

Servings: 3

Ingredients:

- 1 lb. of Red Cabbage, quartered and core removed
- 1 Shallot, thinly sliced
- 2 cloves of Garlic, thinly sliced
- ½ tablespoon of Balsamic Vinegar
- ½ tablespoon of Unsalted Butter
- Salt to taste

Directions:

1. Make a water bath, place Sous Vide cooker in it, and set it to 185 °F.
2. Divide the cabbage and the remaining ingredients into 2 vacuum-sealable bags.
3. Release air by the water displacement method and seal the bags.
4. Submerge them in the water bath and set the timer to cook for 1 hour 30 minutes.
5. Once the timer has stopped, remove and unseal the bag.
6. Transfer the cabbage with juices into serving plates.
7. Season with salt and vinegar to taste.
8. Serve as a side dish.

Nutrition:

- Calories: 129
- Fat: 6 g
- Protein: 2 g

63. NUTS, BEETROOT & CHEESE SALAD

Preparation Time: 15 minutes
Cooking Time: 2 hours 30 seconds
Servings: 3
Ingredients:

- 1 lb. of Beetroot, peeled
- ½ cup of Almonds, blanched
- 2 tablespoons of Hazelnuts, skinned
- 2 teaspoon of Olive Oil
- 1 clove of Garlic, finely minced
- 1 teaspoon of Cumin Powder
- 1 teaspoon of Lemon Zest
- Salt to taste
- ½ cup of Goat Cheese, crumbled
- Fresh Mint Leaves to garnish

<u>Dressing:</u>

- 2 tablespoons of Olive Oil
- 1 tablespoon of Apple Cider Vinegar

Directions:

1. Make a water bath, place the Sous Vide cooker in it, and set it at 183 °F.
2. Cut the beetroots into wedges and bag in a vacuum-sealable bag.
3. Release air by the water displacement method, seal and submerge the bag in the water bath, and set the timer for 2 hours. Once the timer has stopped, remove and unseal the bag. Place the beetroot aside.
4. Put a pan over medium heat, add almonds and hazelnuts, and toast for 3 minutes. Transfer to a cutting board and chop.
5. Add oil to the same pan, garlic, and cumin. Cook for 30 seconds. Turn heat off. In a bowl, combine the goat cheese, almond mixture, and lemon zest and garlic mixture. Mix. Whisk olive oil, vinegar, and place aside. Serve as a side dish.

Nutrition:

- Calories: 127
- Fat: 7 g
- Protein: 7 g

64. CREAMY CAULIFLOWER BROCCOLI SOUP

Preparation Time: 5 minutes

Cooking Time: 2 hours 3 minutes

Servings: 2

Ingredients:

- 1 medium cauliflower, cut into small florets
- ½ lb. of Broccoli, cut into small florets
- 1 Green Bell Pepper, chopped
- 1 medium White Onion, diced
- 1 teaspoon of Olive Oil
- 1 clove of Garlic, crushed
- ½ cup of Vegetable Stock
- ½ cup of Skimmed Milk

Directions:

1. Make a water bath, place the Sous Vide machine in it, and set it to 185 °F.
2. Place the cauliflower, broccoli, bell pepper, and white onion in a vacuum-sealable bag and pour olive oil into it.
3. Release air by the water displacement method and seal the bag. Submerge the bag in the water bath. Set the timer for 50 minutes and cook.
4. Once the timer has stopped, remove the bag and unseal it. Transfer the vegetables to a blender, add garlic and milk, and puree to smooth.
5. Place a pan over medium heat, add the vegetable puree and vegetable stock and simmer for 3 minutes. Season with salt and pepper. Serve warm as a side dish.

Nutrition

- Calories: 102
- Fat: 5.9 g
- Protein: 3 g

65. MEDITERRANEAN EGGPLANT LASAGNA

Preparation Time: 20 minutes
Cooking Time: 2 hours
Servings: 3
Ingredients:

- 1 lb. of Eggplant, peeled and thinly sliced
- 1 tablespoon of Salt
- 1 cup of Tomato Sauce, divided into 3
- 2 oz. of Fresh Mozzarella, thinly sliced
- 1 oz. of Parmesan Cheese, grated
- 2 oz. of Italian Blend Cheese, grated
- 3 tablespoons of Fresh Basil, chopped

Topping:

- ½ tablespoon of Macadamia Nuts, toasted and chopped
- 1 oz. of Parmesan Cheese, grated
- 1 oz. of Italian Blend Cheese, grated

Directions:

1. Make a water bath, place Sous Vide cooker in it, and set it at 183 °F.
2. Place the eggplants in a colander, toss with salt, and let drain for 15 minutes.
3. While water heats, peel eggplants, slice into thin rounds, and toss with salt.
4. Lay a vacuum-sealable bag on its side; make a layer of half the eggplant, spread one portion of tomato sauce, layer mozzarella, then parmesan, then cheese blend, then basil.
5. Top with the second portion of tomato sauce.
6. Seal the bag carefully by the water displacement method, keeping it flat as possible.
7. Submerge the bag flat in the water bath.
8. Set the timer for 2 hours and cook.
9. Release air 2 to 3 times within the first 30 minutes as eggplant releases gas as it cooks.
10. Once the timer has stopped, remove the bag gently and poke one corner of the bag using a pin to release liquid from the bag.
11. Lay the bag flat on a serving plate, cut open the top of it and gently slide the lasagna onto the plate.
12. Top with remaining tomato sauce, macadamia nuts, cheese blend, and Parmesan cheese.
13. Melt and brown the cheese using a torch.

Nutrition:

- Calories: 25
- Fat: 0.2 g
- Protein: 1 g

66. TRADITIONAL RATATOUILLE

Preparation Time: 30 minutes
Cooking Time: 1 hour 50 minutes
Servings: 3
Ingredients:
- 2 medium Zucchini, cut into ¼ inch dices
- 2 medium Tomatoes, cut into ¼ inch dices
- 2 Red Capsicum, seeded and cut into 2-inch dices
- 1 small Eggplant, cut into ¼ inch dices
- 1 Onion, cut into 1-inch dices
- Salt to taste
- ½ Red Pepper Flakes
- 8 cloves Garlic, crushed
- 2 ½ tablespoons of Olive Oil
- 5 sprigs + 2 sprigs of Basil Leaves

Directions:
1. Make a water bath, place a Sous Vide cooker in it, and set it at 185 °F.
2. Place the tomatoes, zucchini, onion, bell pepper, and eggplant each in 5 separate vacuum-sealable bags.
3. Put garlic, basil leaves, and 1 tablespoon of olive oil in each bag.
4. Release air by the water displacement method, seal and submerge the bags in the water bath, and set the timer for 20 minutes.
5. Once the timer has stopped, remove the bag with the tomatoes.
6. Place aside.
7. Reset the timer for 30 minutes.
8. Once the timer has stopped, remove the bags with the zucchinis and red bell peppers. Place aside.
9. Reset the timer for 1 hour.
10. Once the timer has stopped, remove the remaining bags and discard the garlic and basil leaves.
11. In a bowl, add tomatoes and use a spoon to mash them lightly.
12. Roughly, chop the remaining vegetables and add to the tomatoes.
13. Season with salt, red pepper flakes, remaining olive oil, and basil.
14. Serve.

Nutrition:
- Calories: 200
- Protein: 20 g
- Fat: 3 g

67. SPEEDY POACHED TOMATOES

Preparation Time: 5 minutes

Cooking Time: 30 minutes

Servings: 3

Ingredients:

- 4 cups of Cherry Tomatoes
- 5 tablespoons of Olive Oil
- ½ tablespoon of Fresh Rosemary Leaves, minced
- ½ tablespoon of Fresh Thyme Leaves, minced
- Salt to taste
- Pepper to taste

Directions:

1. Make a water bath, place Sous Vide machine in it, and set it to 131 °F.
2. Divide the listed ingredients into 2 vacuum-sealable bags, season with salt and pepper.
3. Release air by the water displacement method and seal the bags.
4. Submerge them in the water bath and set the timer to cook for 30 minutes.
5. Once the timer has stopped, remove the bag and unseal it.
6. Transfer the tomatoes with the juices into a bowl. Serve as a side dish.

Nutrition:

- Calories: 180
- Fat: 16 g
- Protein: 34 g

68. CHILI BRUSSELS SPROUTS IN SWEET SYRUP

Preparation Time: 20 minutes
Cooking Time: 56 minutes
Servings: 3
Ingredients:
- 4 lb. of Brussels sprouts stems trimmed and halved
- 3 tablespoons of Olive Oil
- ¾ cup of Fish Sauce
- 3 tablespoons of Water
- 2 tablespoons of Sugar
- 1 ½ tablespoon of Rice Vinegar
- 2 teaspoon of Lime Juice
- 3 Red Chilies, sliced thinly
- 2 cloves of Garlic, minced
- Salt to taste

Directions:
1. Make a water bath, place a Sous Vide cooker in it, and set it at 183 °F.
2. Pour the brussels sprouts, salt, and oil in a vacuum-sealable bag, release air by the water displacement method, seal and submerge the bag in the water bath. Set the timer for 50 minutes.
3. Once the timer has stopped, remove the bag, unseal it, and transfer the Brussels sprouts to a foiled baking sheet.
4. Preheat a broiler to high, place the baking sheet in it, and broil for 6 minutes. Pour the Brussels sprouts into a bowl.
5. Make the sauce: in a bowl, add the remaining listed cooking ingredients and stir. Add the sauce to the Brussels sprouts and toss evenly. Serve as a side dish.

Nutrition:
- Calories: 43
- Fat: 0.3 g
- Protein: 3.4 g

69. AROMATIC BRAISED BEETROOTS

Preparation Time: 15 minutes

Cooking Time: 1 hour

Servings: 3

Ingredients:

- 2 Beets, peeled and sliced into 1 cm inches
- 1/3 cup of Balsamic Vinegar
- ½ teaspoon of Olive Oil
- 1/3 cup of Toasted Walnuts
- 1/3 cup of Grana Padano Cheese, grated
- Salt to taste
- Pepper to taste

Directions:

1. Make a water bath, place a Sous Vide cooker in it, and set it at 183 °F.
2. Place the beets, vinegar, and salt in a vacuum-sealable bag.
3. Release air by the water displacement method, seal and submerge the bag in the water bath. Set the timer for 1 hour.
4. Once the timer has stopped, remove and unseal the bag.
5. Transfer the beets to a bowl, add olive oil, and toss.
6. Sprinkle walnuts and cheese over it.
7. Serve as a side dish.

Nutrition:

- Calories: 43
- Fat: 0.3 g
- Protein: 1.7 g

70. POMODORO SOUP

Preparation Time: 10 minutes

Cooking Time: 50 minutes

Servings: 3

Ingredients:

- 2 lb. of Tomatoes, halved
- 1 Onion, diced
- 1 Celery Stick, chopped
- 3 tablespoons of Olive Oil
- 1 tablespoon of unsweetened Tomato Puree
- A pinch of Sugar
- 1 Bay Leaf

Directions:

1. Make a water bath, place a Sous Vide cooker in it, and set it at 185 °F.
2. Place all the listed ingredients except the salt in a bowl and toss. Put them in a vacuum-sealable bag.
3. Release air by the water displacement method, seal, and submerge the bag into the water bath. Set the timer for 40 minutes.
4. Once the timer has stopped, remove the bag and unseal it.
5. Puree the ingredients using a blender.
6. Pour the blended tomato into a pot and set it over medium heat. Season with salt and cook for 10 minutes. Dish soup into bowls and cool.

Nutrition:

- Calories: 270
- Fat: 4 g
- Protein: 18 g

71. SIMPLE MUSHROOM SOUP

Preparation Time: 4 minutes
Cooking Time: 40 minutes
Servings: 3
Ingredients:
- 1 lb. of Mixed Mushrooms
- 2 Onions, diced
- 3 cloves of Garlic
- 2 sprigs of Parsley Leaves, chopped
- 2 tablespoons of Thyme Powder
- 2 tablespoons of Olive Oil
- 2 cups of Cream
- 2 cups of Vegetable Stock
- 1 sprigs of celery

Directions:
1. Make a water bath, place a Sous Vide cooker in it, and set it at 185 °F.
2. Place the mushrooms, onion, and celery in a vacuum-sealable bag.
3. Release air by the water displacement method, seal and submerge the bag in the water bath. Set the timer for 30 minutes. Once the timer has stopped, remove and unseal the bag.
4. Blend the ingredients in the bag in a blender. Put a pan over medium heat and add the olive oil. Once it starts to heat, add the pureed mushrooms and the remaining listed ingredients except for the cream. Cook for 10 minutes.
5. Turn off heat and add cream. Stir well. Serve with a side of bread.

Nutrition:
- Calories: 22
- Fat: 0.3 g
- Protein: 3.1 g

72. EASY MIXED VEGETABLE SOUP

Preparation Time: 10 minutes
Cooking Time: 40 minutes
Servings: 3
Ingredients:
- 1 Sweet Onion, sliced
- 1 teaspoon of Garlic Powder
- 2 cups of Zucchini, cut in small dices
- 3 oz. of Parmesan Rind
- 2 cups of Baby Spinach
- 2 tablespoons of Olive Oil
- 1 teaspoon of Red Pepper Flakes
- 2 cups of Vegetable Stock
- 1 sprig of Rosemary
- Salt to taste

Directions:
1. Make a water bath, place a Sous Vide cooker in it, and set it at 185 °F.
2. Toss all the ingredients with olive oil except the garlic and salt, and place them in a vacuum-sealable bag.
3. Release air by water displacement method, seal and submerge the bag in the water bath. Set the timer for 30 minutes.
4. Once the timer has stopped, remove and unseal the bag. Discard the rosemary. Pour the remaining ingredients into a pot and add the salt and garlic powder.
5. Once the timer has stopped, remove and unseal the bag. Discard the rosemary. Pour the remaining ingredients into a pot and add the salt and garlic powder.
6. Put the pot over medium heat and simmer for 10 minutes. Serve as a light dish.

Nutrition:
- Calories: 150
- Fat: 0.3 g
- Protein: 1.2 g

73. POWER GREEN SOUP

Preparation Time: 10 minutes
Cooking Time: 40 minutes
Servings: 3
Ingredients:

- 4 cups of Vegetable Stock
- 1 tablespoon of Olive Oil
- 1 clove of Garlic, crushed
- 1-inch Ginger, sliced
- 1 teaspoon of Coriander Powder
- 1 large Zucchini, diced
- 3 cups of Kale
- 2 cups of Broccoli, cut into florets
- 1 lime, juiced, and zest
- 2 sprigs of Parsley

Directions:

1. Make a water bath, place a Sous Vide cooker in it, and set it at 185 °F.
2. Place the broccoli, zucchini, kale, and parsley in a vacuum-sealable bag.
3. Release air by the water displacement method, seal and submerge the bag in the water bath. Set the timer for 30 minutes.
4. Once the timer has stopped, remove and unseal the bag. Add the steamed ingredients to a blender with garlic and ginger. Puree to smooth.
5. Pour the green puree into a pot and add the remaining listed ingredients.
6. Put the pot over medium heat and simmer for 10 minutes. Serve as a light dish.

Nutrition:

- Calories: 153
- Fat: 1 g
- Protein: 6 g

74. SIMPLE HARD-BOILED EGGS

Preparation Time: 10 minutes

Cooking Time: 1 hour

Servings: 6

Ingredients:

- 6 large Eggs
- Ice bath

Directions:

1. Make a water bath, place a Sous Vide cooker in it, and set it at 165 °F.
2. Place the eggs in the water bath and set the timer for 1 hour.
3. Once the timer has stopped, transfer the eggs to the ice bath.
4. Peel eggs. Serve as a snack or in salads.

Nutrition:

- Calories: 78
- Fat: 5.3 g
- Protein: 6.3 g

75. COLORFUL BELL PEPPER MIX

Preparation Time: 20 minutes

Cooking Time: 15 minutes

Servings: 2

Ingredients:

- 1 Red Bell Pepper, chopped
- 1 Yellow Bell Pepper, chopped
- 1 Green Bell Pepper, chopped
- 1 Large Orange Bell Pepper, chopped
- Salt to taste

Directions:

1. Make a water bath, place a Sous Vide cooker in it, and set it at 183 °F.
2. Place all the bell peppers with salt in a vacuum-sealable bag.
3. Release air by the water displacement method, seal and submerge in the water bath.
4. Set the timer for 15 minutes.
5. Once the timer has stopped, remove and unseal the bag.
6. Serve bell peppers with their juices as a side dish.

Nutrition:

- Calories: 31
- Fat: 0.4 g
- Protein: 1 g

76. CILANTRO CURRIED ZUCCHINIS

Preparation Time: 10 minutes

Cooking Time: 25 minutes

Servings: 3

Ingredients:

- 3 small Zucchinis, diced
- 2 teaspoon of Curry Powder
- 1 tablespoon of Olive Oil
- Salt to taste
- Pepper to taste
- ¼ cup of Cilantro

Directions:

1. Make a water bath, place a Sous Vide cooker in it, and set it at 185 °F.
2. Place the zucchinis in a vacuum-sealable bag.
3. Release air by the water displacement method, seal and submerge the bag in the water bath. Set the timer for 20 minutes.
4. Once the timer has stopped, remove and unseal the bag.
5. Place a skillet over medium and add the olive oil.
6. Once it has been heated, add the zucchinis and the remaining listed ingredients.
7. Season with salt and stir-fry for 5 minutes.
8. Serve.

Nutrition:

- Calories: 17
- Fat: 0.3 g
- Protein: 1.2 g

77. PAPRIKA BELL PEPPER PUREE

Preparation Time: 20 minutes

Cooking Time: 23 minutes

Servings: 4

Ingredients:

- 8 Red Bell Peppers, cored
- 1/3 cup of Olive Oil
- 2 tablespoons of Lemon Juice
- 3 cloves of Garlic, crushed
- 2 teaspoon of Sweet Paprika

Directions:

1. Make a water bath, place a Sous Vide cooker in it, and set it at 183 °F.
2. Put the bell peppers, garlic, and olive oil in a vacuum-sealable bag.
3. Release air by the water displacement method, seal and submerge the bags in the water bath. Set the timer for 20 minutes and cook.
4. Once the timer has stopped, remove the bag and unseal it. Transfer the bell pepper and garlic to a blender and puree to smooth.
5. Place a pan over medium heat; add bell pepper puree and the remaining listed ingredients. Cook for 3 minutes. Serve warm or cold as a dip.

Nutrition:

- Calories: 20
- Fat: 0.2 g
- Protein: 0.9 g

78. ARTICHOKE HEARTS WITH GREEN CHILIES

Preparation Time: 1 hour 15 minutes
Cooking Time: 33 minutes
Servings: 6
Ingredients:

- 2 Onions, quartered
- 3 cloves of Garlic, minced
- 15 oz. of Artichoke Hearts, soaked for 1 hour, drained, and chopped
- 18 oz. of Frozen Spinach, thawed
- 5 oz. of Green Chilies
- 3 tablespoons of Olive Oil Mayonnaise
- 3 tablespoons of Whipped Cream Cheese
- Salt and Pepper to taste
- ½ cup of lemon juice

Directions:

1. Make a water bath, place a Sous Vide cooker in it, and set it at 181 °F. Divide the onions, garlic, artichoke hearts, spinach, and green chilies into 2 vacuum-sealable bags.
2. Release air by the water displacement method, seal and submerge the bags in the water bath. Set the timer for 30 minutes to cook.
3. Once the timer has stopped, remove and unseal the bag. Puree the ingredients using a blender. Place a pan over medium heat and add the butter.
4. Once it has melted, add the vegetable puree, lemon juice, olive oil mayonnaise, and cream cheese. Season with salt and pepper. Stir and cook for 3 minutes. Serve warm with a side of vegetable strips.

Nutrition:

- Calories: 47
- Fat: 0.2 g
- Protein: 3.3 g

79. CHILI & GARLIC SAUCE

Preparation Time: 7 minutes

Cooking Time: 30 minutes

Servings: 15

Ingredients:

- 2 lb. of Red Chili Peppers
- 4 cloves of Garlic, crushed
- 2 teaspoon of Smoked Paprika
- 1 cup of Cilantro Leaves, chopped
- ½ cup of Basil Leaves, chopped
- 2 Lemons Juice

Directions:

1. Make a water bath, place a Sous Vide cooker in it, and set it at 185 °F.
2. Place the peppers in a vacuum-sealable bag.
3. Release air by the water displacement method, seal and submerge the bag in the water bath. Set the timer for 30 minutes.
4. Once the timer has stopped, remove and unseal the bag.
5. Transfer the pepper and the remaining listed ingredients to a blender and puree to smooth.
6. Store in an airtight container, refrigerate and use for up to 7 days.

Nutrition:

- Calories: 25
- Fat: 0.2 g
- Protein: 0.9 g

80. PARMESAN GARLIC ASPARAGUS

Preparation Time: 6 minutes
Cooking Time: 16 minutes
Serving: 4
Ingredients:

- 1 bunch of green asparagus, trimmed
- 4 tablespoons of unsalted butter, cut into cubes
- Sea salt
- 1 tablespoon of pressed garlic
- 1/4 cup of shaved Parmesan cheese

Directions:

1. Preheat your sous vide to 185 °F or 85 °C.
2. Place the asparagus in a single layer row in the bag or bags you're going to use to sous vide. Put a tablespoon of butter in each of the corners, the pressed garlic in the middle, salt to taste, and seal the bag. Move the bag around to get garlic to disperse evenly.
3. Place the bag in your preheated water and set the timer for 14 minutes.
4. Top the cooked asparagus with some of the liquid from the bag and the parmesan cheese.
5. Serve immediately.

Nutrition:

- Calories: 85
- Fat: 1 g
- Protein: 0.9 g

81. BLACKENED BRUSSELS SPROUTS WITH GARLIC AND BACON

Preparation Time: 16 minutes
Cooking Time: 85 minutes
Serving: 8
Ingredients:

- 2 lbs. of Brussels sprouts
- 3 cloves of garlic, chopped
- 3 strips of bacon
- Bacon fat, from cooking the bacon
- Salt and pepper

Directions:

1. Preheat your sous vide to 183 °F or 83.9 °C.
2. Wash the Brussels sprouts and use paper towels to pat them dry.
3. Heat a skillet on medium heat for a few min. When it's hot, add in the bacon. Cook the bacon until crispy, flipping halfway through. Remove the bacon and add in the garlic.
4. Cook the garlic in the pan with the bacon fat until fragrant, about 1 minute. Then place the bacon, fat, and garlic in a bowl.
5. Put the Brussels sprouts in the bag or bags you're going to use to sous-vide along with the bacon fat, a little fresh ground pepper, and garlic. Shake the bag around so everything is well mixed, and seal the bag.
6. Place the bag in your preheated water and set the timer for 50 minutes.
7. At the 35-minute mark, preheat your oven to 400 °F and line a large rimmed baking sheet with parchment paper.
8. Place the cooked mixture on the baking sheet, ensuring the Brussels sprouts are in a single layer. Put the baking sheet in the oven and cook the Brussels sprouts for 5 to 7 min. The sprouts should blacken a little bit when they're ready.
9. Serve immediately.

Nutrition:

- Calories: 105
- Fat: 6 g
- Protein: 9 g

82. ASIAN INSPIRED BOK CHOY

Preparation Time: 11 minutes
Cooking Time: 30 minutes
Serving: 4
Ingredients:

- 1 tablespoon of Ginger, Minced
- 2 Cloves Garlic, Minced
- 1 tablespoon of Toasted Sesame Oil
- 1 tablespoon of Canola Oil
- 1 tablespoon of Soy Sauce
- 1 tablespoon of Fish Sauce
- 1 teaspoon of Red Pepper Flake
- 1 lb. of Baby Bok Choy, Cut in Half Lengthwise
- 1 tablespoon of Toasted Sesame Seed
- 1 tablespoon of Cilantro Leaves

Directions:

1. Preheat your sous vide to 176 °F or 80 °C.
2. Put the garlic and ginger in a large heatproof container.
3. Put the sesame oil and canola oil in a small pot and heat it on medium heat. You want the oil to get so hot that it just starts to smoke.
4. Take the pot off the heat and pour it into the container with the garlic and ginger.
5. Mix in the bok choy, red pepper flakes, fish sauce, and soy sauce.
6. Place the entire mixture in the bag you're going to use to sous vide and seal the bag.
7. Place the bag in your preheated water and set the timer for 20 minutes.
8. Place the cooked bok choy on a plate or in a bowl, and top with the cilantro and sesame seeds.
9. Serve immediately.

Nutrition:

- Calories: 98
- Fat: 1 g
- Protein: 9 g

83. ROSEMARY AND GARLIC POTATOES

Preparation Time: 6 minutes

Cooking Time: 60 minutes

Serving: 4

Ingredients:

- 8 to 10 red-skinned new potatoes, scrubbed, rinsed, and quartered
- Coarse salt
- Freshly ground black pepper
- Garlic powder
- 2 teaspoon of fresh rosemary, finely minced
- 1 tablespoon of olive oil
- 1 tablespoon of rendered bacon or duck fat, or unsalted butter (optional)

Directions:

1. Preheat your sous vide to 183 °F or 83.9 °C.
2. Place the potatoes in a bowl and drizzle them with a little olive oil, just enough to coat them. Toss the potatoes to ensure every part is coated with oil. Season with the 2 teaspoons of rosemary, salt, pepper, and garlic powder to taste. Toss the potatoes again.
3. Place the butter or fat if using in bag or bags you're going to use to sous-vide along with the potatoes seal the bag.
4. Place the bag in your preheated water and set the timer for 1 hour.
5. Place the cooked potatoes in a bowl or on a plate.
6. Serve immediately.

Nutrition:

- Calories: 65
- Fat: 5 g
- Protein: 11 g

84. CANDED SWEET POTATOES

Preparation Time: 6 minutes

Cooking Time: 90 minutes

Serving: 6

Ingredients:

- 4 cups of sweet potatoes, peeled and cubed into ½ inch pieces
- 4 tablespoons of unsalted butter, cut into small pieces
- 4 tablespoons of brown sugar
- 1 teaspoon of ginger root, finely minced
- 1 pinch of cinnamon
- 1 pinch of cayenne pepper
- 1 pinch of ground clove
- Salt and pepper to taste
- 1 cup of mini marshmallows
- 1 to 2 tablespoons of brown sugar, optional addition for topping

Directions:

1. Preheat your sous vide to 183 °F or 83.9 °C.
2. Put the sweet potatoes in the bag you're going to use to sous-vide along with the butter, ginger, cinnamon, cayenne, clove, and salt and pepper. Massage the bag to disperse the butter evenly and seal it.
3. Place the bag in your preheated water and set the timer for 1 hour 30 minutes.
4. Place the cooked sweet potatoes in a bowl and top with brown sugar and marshmallows.
5. Serve immediately.

Nutrition:

- Calories: 115
- Fat: 11 g
- Protein: 9 g

CHAPTER 10.   EGG RECIPES

85. SMOKED FISH AND POACHED EGG

Preparation Time: 14 minutes

Cooking Time: 20 minutes

Serving: 4

Ingredients:

- 4 fillets of smoked fish
- 2 lemons, cut into slices
- Seasonings of your choice
- 4 large eggs
- 4 tablespoons of olive oil

Directions:

1. Follow the instructions given in the manual and fill the sous vide water oven. Preheat it to 140 °F.
2. Divide all the ingredients except eggs into 4 vacuum-seal pouches or Ziploc bags.
3. Seal the pouches, but do not remove the air completely.
4. Submerge both pouches in the water bath and set the timer for 20 minutes.
5. When the timer goes off, remove the pouches and set them aside.
6. Increase the temperature to 167 °F.
7. Place the eggs on a spoon, one at a time, and gently lower them into the water bath, and place them on the lower rack. Set the timer for 15 minutes.
8. Empty each pouch onto individual serving plates. Break an egg over each fillet and serve.

Nutrition:

- Calories: 419
- Fat: 29 g
- Protein: 15 g

86. BRIOCHE AND EGGS

Preparation Time: 13 minutes

Cooking Time: 46 minutes

Serving: 6

Ingredients:

- 6 brioche buns
- 6 large eggs
- 2 scallions, sliced (optional)
- 1 ½ cups of grated cheese

Directions:

1. Follow the instructions given in the manual and fill the sous vide water oven. Preheat it to 149 °F.
2. Place the eggs on a spoon, one at a time, and gently lower them into the water bath, and place them on the rack. Set the timer for 45 minutes.
3. When the timer goes off, immediately remove the eggs from the water bath. Place the eggs in a bowl of cold water for a few minutes.
4. Place brioche buns on a baking sheet and break a cooked egg on each bun. Sprinkle cheese on top.
5. Set an oven to broil and place the baking sheet in the oven. Broil for few minutes until cheese melts.

Nutrition:

- Calories: 397
- Fat: 34 g
- Protein: 19 g

87. EGG BITES

Preparation Time: 9 minutes

Cooking Time: 60 minutes

Serving: 4

Ingredient

- 5 eggs
- ¼ cup of shredded Colby Jack cheese
- 3 tablespoons of unsweetened almond milk
- Salt to taste
- Pepper to taste

Directions:

1. Follow the instructions given in the manual and fill the sous vide water oven. Preheat it to 172 °F.
2. Add a tablespoon of cheese into each of 4 canning jars or Mason jars.
3. Whisk together eggs and milk in a bowl. Divide the egg mixture among the jars. Season with salt and pepper.
4. Fasten the lid lightly, not very tight.
5. Submerge the canning jars in a water bath and adjust the timer for 1 hour or until eggs are set.
6. Remove the jars from the water bath. Serve directly from the jars.

Nutrition:

- Calories: 392
- Fat: 22 g
- Protein: 13 g

88. SOUS VIDE SCRAMBLED EGGS

Preparation Time: 9 minutes

Cooking Time: 12 minutes

Serving: 4

Ingredients:

- 8 large eggs
- Freshly ground pepper to taste
- Salt to taste
- Aleppo pepper to taste (optional)
- 2 tablespoons of butter

Directions:

1. Follow the instructions given in the manual and fill the sous vide water oven. Preheat it to 165 °F.
2. Add the eggs, salt, and pepper into a bowl and whisk well. Pour into a large silicone bag, and vacuum seal the pouch.
3. Submerge the pouch in the water bath and adjust the timer for 10 minutes.
4. Remove the pouch from the water bath and place the pouch between your palms. Press it and shake it.
5. Place it back in the water bath. Set the timer for 12 minutes.
6. When the timer goes off, remove the pouch from the water bath.
7. Open the pouch and divide it into 4 plates.
8. Garnish with Aleppo pepper. Serve immediately.

Nutrition:

- Calories: 384
- Fat: 28 g
- Protein: 13 g

89. EGG WITH SUNCHOKES VELOUTÉ, CRISPY PROSCIUTTO AND HAZELNUT

Preparation Time: 7 minutes
Cooking Time: 49 minutes
Serving: 3
Ingredients:

For Sunchokes Velouté:

- 2 tablespoons of butter
- 1 small leek, only white part, thinly sliced
- 1 pound of Jerusalem artichokes (Sunchokes), peeled
- ½ quart of milk
- ¼ cup of heavy cream (optional)
- 1 medium onion, thinly sliced
- 1 clove of garlic, sliced
- ½ quart of chicken stock
- ¼ vanilla of bean, scraped

For bouquet garni:

- 2 or 3 thyme sprigs
- 2 or 3 fresh sage leaves
- 1 bay leaf
- Leek greens to wrap

For sous vide eggs:

- 3 eggs, at room temperature

For finishing:

- 3 thin slices of prosciutto

- Few strips fried Jerusalem artichokes (sunchokes)
- A handful of baby watercress
- 6 hazelnuts, toasted, chopped
- Oil, as required

Directions:

1. Follow the instructions given in the manual and fill the sous vide water oven. Preheat it to 145 °F.
2. Place the eggs on a spoon and gently lower them into the water bath. Place on the lower rack. Set the timer for 47 minutes.
3. Meanwhile, make the sunchoke velouté as follows: Place a casserole dish over medium flame. Add butter. When butter melts, add onion, garlic, leeks, salt, and pepper.
4. To make bouquet garni, place together thyme, sage, and bay leaf and wrap it with leek greens.
5. Place bouquet garni in the casserole dish. Cook for a few minutes.
6. Stir in the artichokes and cook until slightly tender. Stir occasionally.
7. Add the rest of the ingredients and stir. Once it boils, reduce the flame and let it simmer until tender. Turn off the heat and remove the bouquet garni.
8. Blend the mixture in a blender. Strain the mixture through a wire mesh strainer placed over a saucepan.
9. To finish: smear the oil over the prosciutto slices and lay them on a lined baking sheet.
10. Bake in a preheated oven at 300 °F until crisp. Remove from the oven and cool.
11. Place a few strips of sunchoke on a nonstick pan. Add a bit of oil. Add the sunchoke and cook until crisp. Sprinkle salt.
12. Crack a cooked egg into each of 3 bowls.
13. Spoon the sunchoke velouté over the eggs in each bowl.
14. Serve topped with prosciutto, hazelnuts, watercress, and fried sunchoke strips.

Nutrition:

- Calories: 434
- Fat: 31 g
- Protein: 18 g

90. SAUSAGE SCRAMBLE

Preparation Time: 11 minutes

Cooking Time: 20 minutes

Serving: 3

Ingredients:

- 16 large eggs, well beaten
- 8 ounces of breakfast sausages, crumbled
- 4 tablespoons of butter
- Salt and pepper, as per taste
- ½ cup of Mexican cheese, grated

Directions:

1. Follow the instructions given in the manual and fill the sous vide water oven. Preheat it to 165 °F.
2. Place a skillet over medium heat and cook the sausages until they are browned.
3. Transfer the cooked sausages to a bowl lined with paper towels and allow them to cool. Once the sausages cool, place them in a Ziploc bag. Add the eggs, butter, cheese, salt, and pepper and vacuum seal the bag.
4. Submerge and cook in the sous vide cooker for around 20 minutes. Take the pouch out occasionally and shake the contents well before submerging again. Cook until the eggs are as per your liking.
5. Remove from the water bath and serve.

Nutrition:

- Calories: 384
- Fat: 34 g
- Protein: 21 g

91. EGGS BENEDICT

Preparation Time: 13 minutes
Cooking Time: 60 minutes
Serving: 4
Ingredients:
- 4 English muffins, halved, toasted
- 8 slices of Canadian bacon
- A handful of fresh parsley, chopped
- 8 eggs
- Butter, as required

For hollandaise sauce:
- 8 tablespoons of butter
- 2 teaspoons of lemon juice
- 1 shallot, diced
- Salt to taste
- Cayenne pepper to taste
- 2 egg yolks
- 2 teaspoons of water

Directions:
1. Follow the instructions given in the manual and fill the sous vide water oven. Preheat it to 148 °F.
2. Place the eggs in a vacuum-seal pouch or Ziploc bag. Place all the ingredients for hollandaise sauce into another bag. Vacuum seal the pouches.
3. Submerge both pouches in the water bath and set the timer for 1 hour.
4. Meanwhile, cook the bacon in a pan to the desired doneness. Keep warm in an oven along with muffins if desired.
5. Remove the pouches from the water bath. Transfer the contents of the sauce into a blender and blend until smooth.
6. Place muffins on individual serving plates. Crack an egg on each muffin and place it on the bottom half of the muffins.
7. Spoon hollandaise over the eggs and garnish with parsley. Cover with the top half of the muffins and serve.

Nutrition:
- Calories: 344
- Fat: 21 g
- Protein: 19 g

CHAPTER 11.   APPETIZER AND SNACK RECIPES

92. BUFFALO CHICKEN WINGS

Preparation Time: 11 minutes
Cooking Time: 30 minutes
Serving: 4
Ingredients:

- 2 pounds of whole chicken wings
- 1/2 cup of butter
- 1 cup of hot sauce (add another 1/2 cup if you like it hot)
- 1 teaspoon of Worcestershire sauce
- 1 teaspoon of garlic salt
- 1 teaspoon of freshly ground black pepper
- 1/2 cup of all-purpose flour

Directions:
1. Cut the chicken wings into 3 pieces. Keep the drumettes and wingettes (flats), but throw away the wingtips.
2. Fill the water bath with water. Set your sous vide machine temperature to 176 °F.
3. Place the chicken wing pieces in a food-safe bag and vacuum seal the bag. Make sure they are lined up side by side and not stacked or piled. Use multiple bags if necessary.
4. Place the chicken wings in the water bath, and cook sous vide for 3 hours.
5. To make the buffalo sauce, melt the butter in a medium saucepan over medium heat. Add all the remaining ingredients except the flour and simmer for about 10 minutes, stirring often.
6. Prepare a Dutch oven or deep fryer with oil; preheat oil to 350 °F.
7. Remove the chicken wings from the bag and pat dry with a paper towel.
8. Dredge the wings in flour. Shake off excess flour and deep-fry the chicken in 350 °F oil for about 8–10 minutes.
9. Place the wings on paper towels to remove the excess oil and then toss them with buffalo sauce.

Nutrition:

- Calories: 344
- Fat: 21 g
- Protein: 19 g

93. HONEY GARLIC CHICKEN WINGS

Preparation Time: 11 minutes
Cooking Time: 33 minutes
Serving: 4
Ingredients:

- 2 pounds of whole chicken wings
- 1/3 cup of butter
- 8–10 cloves garlic, minced
- 1/2 cup of soy sauce
- 1 cup of honey
- 2 teaspoons of water
- 1 teaspoon of cornstarch
- 1/2 cup of all-purpose flour

Directions:

1. Cut the chicken wings into 3 pieces. Keep the drumettes and wingettes (flats), but throw away the wingtips.
2. Fill the water bath with water. Set your sous vide machine temperature to 176 °F.
3. Place the chicken wing pieces in a food-safe bag and vacuum seal the bag. Make sure they are lined up side by side and not stacked or piled. Use multiple bags if necessary.
4. Place the wings in the water bath, and cook sous vide for 3 hours.
5. To make the sauce, melt the butter in a medium saucepan over medium heat. Add the minced garlic and cook for 2–3 minutes to release the flavor.
6. Add the soy sauce and honey and bring to a boil. Lower the heat to a simmer.
7. In a small bowl, whisk together the water and cornstarch to make a slurry. Whisk the slurry into the honey sauce and continue to stir as the sauce thickens over the next 3–4 minutes.
8. Prepare a Dutch oven or deep fryer with oil; preheat oil to 350 °F.
9. Remove the chicken wings from the bag and pat dry with a paper towel.
10. Dredge the wings in flour. Shake off the excess flour and deep-fry the wings in 350 °F oil for about 8–10 minutes.
11. Place the wings on paper towels to remove the excess oil and toss them with the honey garlic sauce.

Nutrition:

- Calories: 381
- Fat: 25 g
- Protein: 19 g

94. HUMMUS

Preparation Time: 11 minutes
Cooking Time: 3 hours
Serving: 6
Ingredients:

- 1/2 cup of dried chickpeas
- 2 cups of water, divided
- 2 cloves of garlic, divided
- 1 tablespoon of lemon juice
- 2 tablespoons of tahini
- 1/2 teaspoon of sea salt
- 2 tablespoons of extra-virgin olive oil
- 1 teaspoon of ground cumin

Directions:

1. Fill the water bath with water. Set your sous vide machine temperature to 195 °F.
2. Place the chickpeas, 1 1/2 cups of water, and 1 clove of garlic in a large food-safe zip-top bag. Slowly lower the zip-top bag into the water, and, using the water displacement method, the air will escape from the bag. Continue to lower the bag until it is about 1" from being fully submerged. Once the bag has been lowered, zip it shut with your fingers.
3. Cook sous vide for 3 1/2 hours. Check to see if chickpeas are tender and cook longer if needed.
4. Drain the chickpeas and let them cool until they come to room temperature.
5. Using a food processor, pulse the chickpeas, lemon juice, remaining garlic clove, tahini, salt, oil, and cumin. While the food processor is running, slowly pour in the remaining water. Check the texture and thickness of the hummus. If needed, add more water to reach the desired consistency.
6. When ready to serve, scoop the hummus into a small serving bowl and serve with pita bread, crackers, or fresh vegetables.

Nutrition:

- Calories: 244
- Fat: 11 g
- Protein: 9 g

95. BABA GHANOUJ

Preparation Time: 9 minutes

Cooking Time: 3 hours

Serving: 6

Ingredients:

- 1 large eggplant, peeled and cubed
- 1 tablespoon of lemon juice
- 2 cloves of garlic
- 2 tablespoons of tahini
- 1 teaspoon of sea salt
- 2 tablespoons of extra-virgin olive oil
- 2 tablespoons of chopped fresh cilantro

Directions:

1. Fill the water bath with water. Set your sous vide machine temperature to 185°F.
2. Place the cubed eggplant in a food-safe bag and vacuum seal the bag. Make sure the eggplant is in only 1–2 layers within the bag. Use multiple bags if necessary.
3. Place the eggplant in the water bath, and cook sous vide for 2–3 hours.
4. Using a food processor, pulse the cooked eggplant, lemon juice, garlic, tahini, salt, and olive oil. Process until smooth and creamy.
5. Add the cilantro and pulse a few times or until it is evenly mixed throughout the dip. Serve.

Nutrition:

- Calories: 194
- Fat: 19 g
- Protein: 10 g

96. WHITE BEAN AND ARTICHOKE DIP

Preparation Time: 10 minutes
Cooking Time: 4 hours
Serving: 6
Ingredients:

- 1/2 cup of dried cannellini beans
- 11/2 cups of water
- 2 cloves of garlic, divided
- 1 (14-ounces) can of artichoke hearts, drained
- 2 tablespoons of lemon juice
- 2 tablespoons of extra-virgin olive oil
- 1/2 teaspoon of sea salt
- 1/3 cup of grated Parmesan cheese

Directions:

1. Fill the water bath with water. Set your sous vide machine temperature to 195 °F.
2. Place the beans, 11/2 cups of water, and 1 clove of garlic in a large food-safe zip-top bag. Slowly lower the zip-top bag into the water and, using the water displacement method, the air will escape from the bag. Continue to lower the bag until it is about 1" from being fully submerged. Once the bag has been lowered, zip it shut with your fingers.
3. Cook sous vide for 3 1/2 hours. Check to see if the beans are tender and cook a little longer if needed.
4. Drain the beans and let them cool until they come to room temperature.
5. Using a food processor, pulse the beans, artichoke hearts, lemon juice, remaining garlic clove, oil, salt, and Parmesan cheese. Process until smooth and creamy. If a thinner consistency is desired, add a little extra water while processing. Serve.

Nutrition:

- Calories: 304
- Fat: 20 g
- Protein: 13 g

97. SHRIMP AND AVOCADO SALSA

Preparation Time: 11 minutes

Cooking Time: 46 minutes

Serving: 6

Ingredients:

- 1-pound of raw medium shrimp, peeled and deveined
- 1 tablespoon of olive oil
- 2 medium avocados, peeled, cored, and cubed
- 3 medium tomatoes, diced
- 2 medium jalapeño peppers, cored and minced
- 1/4 cup of chopped fresh cilantro
- Juice of 2 medium limes
- 1/2 teaspoon of sea salt

Directions:

1. Fill the water bath with water. Set your sous vide machine temperature to 140 °F.
2. Place the shrimp and olive oil in a food-safe bag and vacuum seal the bag.
3. Place the shrimp in the water bath, and cook sous vide for 30 minutes.
4. Remove the shrimp from the bag and cut each into 2–3 pieces.
5. In a large mixing bowl, combine all the ingredients and toss.
6. Let the salsa marinate, in the refrigerator, for 10–15 minutes before serving.

Nutrition:

- Calories: 249
- Fat: 26 g
- Protein: 15 g

98. TOMATO AND MANGO SALSA

Preparation Time: 11 minutes

Cooking Time: 16 minutes

Serving: 6

Ingredients:

- 2 tablespoons of extra-virgin olive oil
- 3 medium of tomatoes, diced
- 2 large ripe mangos, peeled, pitted, and diced
- 1 medium red onion, diced
- 2 tablespoons of chopped fresh cilantro
- 1 tablespoon of minced fresh mint
- Juice of 1 medium lime
- 1 tablespoon of granulated sugar
- 1/2 teaspoon of sea salt

Directions:

1. Fill the water bath with water. Set your sous vide machine temperature to 150 °F.
2. Place the oil, tomatoes, mangos, and red onion in a food-safe bag and vacuum seal the bag.
3. Place the bag in the water bath, and cook sous vide for 1 hour. Quick chill the bag by placing it in an ice bath.
4. Empty the bag into a large bowl and toss well with the remaining ingredients. Let the salsa marinate, in the refrigerator, for 10–15 minutes before serving.

Nutrition:

- Calories: 264
- Fat: 20 g
- Protein: 13 g

99. SHRIMP AND JALAPEÑO QUESADILLA

Preparation Time: 12 minutes
Cooking Time: 50 minutes
Serving: 8
Ingredients:
- 1-pound of raw medium shrimp, peeled and deveined
- 1 tablespoon of olive oil
- 2 jalapeño peppers, cored and minced
- 3 green onions, sliced
- 3 tablespoons of minced fresh cilantro
- 2 tablespoons of lime juice
- 1/2 teaspoon of sea salt
- 6–8 (8") soft flour tortillas
- 1 cup of grated Cheddar cheese
- 1 cup of grated Monterey jack cheese

Directions:
1. Fill the water bath with water. Set your sous vide machine temperature to 140 °F.
2. Place the shrimp and olive oil in a food-safe bag and vacuum seal the bag.
3. Place the shrimp in the water bath, and cook sous vide for 30 minutes.
4. Preheat oven to 350 °F.
5. Remove the shrimp from the bag and cut each into 2–3 pieces.
6. Place the shrimp and the jalapeño, green onions, cilantro, lime juice, and salt in a large bowl and toss to combine.
7. To make the quesadillas: scoop some of the shrimp mixtures onto half of a soft tortilla. Evenly sprinkle some of each cheese onto the shrimp mixture and then fold the soft tortilla over, covering the shrimp and cheese. Repeat with all the quesadillas.
8. Bake the quesadillas in the oven until the cheese melts and the tortillas are brown, about 10 minutes.
9. Cut each quesadilla into 4 wedges and serve with salsa

Nutrition:
- Calories: 294
- Fat: 29 g
- Protein: 19 g

100. DEEP-FRIED PORK BELLY SKEWERS WITH HONEY GARLIC GLAZE

Preparation Time: 8 minutes

Cooking Time: 16 minutes

Serving: 8

Ingredients:

- 1/3 cup of butter
- 8 cloves of garlic, minced
- 2 medium Thai chilies, sliced
- 1/2 cup of soy sauce
- 1 cup of honey
- 1 pound of 24-Hour Sous Vide Pork Belly
- 12–16 small skewers
- 1 tablespoon of vegetable oil

Directions:

1. First, make the glaze: melt the butter in a small saucepan over medium heat. Add the minced garlic and chilies and cook for 2–3 minutes to release the flavor. Add the soy sauce and honey and bring to a boil. Lower the heat to a simmer. The sauce will thicken after 10 minutes or so.
2. Slice the pork belly into 1" chunks. Spear the chunks onto the skewers.
3. Add the oil to a deep, heavy pan or deep fryer and heat to 325 °F. Slowly place the skewered pork belly in the hot oil and cook for about 4 minutes. The outside should be crispy and golden in color.
4. Remove the pork from the oil and drain on paper towels for 1–2 minutes.
5. Place the pork on a serving plate and drizzle with the honey garlic glaze.

Nutrition:

- Calories: 384
- Fat: 32 g
- Protein: 18 g

101. TOMATO CONFIT AND PROVOLONE GRILLED CHEESE SANDWICH WEDGES

Preparation Time: 9 minutes

Cooking Time: 5 hours

Serving: 6

Ingredients:

- 2 pints of cherry tomatoes
- 1/4 cup of olive oil
- 1 1/2 tablespoons of balsamic vinegar
- 1/2 teaspoon of sea salt
- 1/2 teaspoon of black pepper
- 1/4 cup of butter or margarine, softened
- 8 slices of fresh bread
- 8 slices of provolone or mozzarella cheese
- 1/3 cup of thinly sliced fresh basil

Directions:

1. Fill the water bath with water. Set your sous vide machine temperature to 150 °F.
2. Place the tomatoes, olive oil, vinegar, sea salt, and black pepper in a food-safe bag and vacuum seal the bag.
3. Place the tomatoes in the water bath, and cook sous vide for 4 hours.
4. Remove the tomatoes from the water bath and cool to room temperature. Strain the oil and peel the skins off the tomatoes. The skins should peel off easily.
5. Butter 1 side of each slice of bread. Assemble the sandwiches by laying out a slice of bread buttered side down. Place a slice of cheese on the bread. Put some tomatoes on top of the cheese and sprinkle with fresh basil. Add another slice of cheese and finish the sandwich with another bread slice, buttered side on the outside.

6. Place the sandwiches in a large skillet over medium heat. Cook until golden brown on each side, about 4 minutes per side. Cut the sandwiches into wedges and serve.

Nutrition:

- Calories: 464
- Fat: 26 g
- Protein: 13 g

102. FLANK STEAK, APRICOT, AND BRIE BITES

Preparation Time: 13 minutes

Cooking Time: 18 hours

Serving: 6

Ingredients:

- 1 flank steak (about 2 pounds)
- 1 teaspoon of sea salt
- 1 teaspoon of freshly ground black pepper
- 1 teaspoon of paprika
- 1 medium wheel Brie
- 10–12 dried apricots
- 20–24 fresh mint leaves

Directions:

1. Fill the water bath with water. Set your sous vide machine temperature to 135 °F.
2. Rub the flank steak all over with salt, pepper, and paprika. Place the steak in a food-safe bag and vacuum seal the bag.
3. Place the steak in the water bath, and cook sous vide for 12–18 hours.
4. Remove from the water bath and immediately place in an ice bath to chill the steak. Cut the flank steak, against the grain, into thin slices.
5. Cut the Brie cheese into small slices and cut the dried apricots in half.
6. Assemble the bites by placing a mint leaf and dried apricot half on a piece of sliced Brie. Wrap with a slice of flank steak and pierce with a toothpick. Keep them in the fridge until ready to serve.

Nutrition:

- Calories: 549
- Fat: 31 g
- Protein: 16 g

103. PORK TENDERLOIN, TOMATO, AND BOCCONCINI CANAPÉS

Preparation Time: 13 minutes
Cooking Time: 3 hours
Serving: 4
Ingredients:

- 1/2 teaspoon of sea salt
- 1/2 teaspoon of freshly ground black pepper
- 1 pork of tenderloin (about 1 pound)
- 1 tablespoon of oil with a high smoke point (like peanut, sunflower, corn, vegetable, or safflower oil)
- 1 baguette, sliced and lightly toasted
- 3–4 plum or Roma tomatoes, sliced
- 1 (8-ounces) container of Bocconcini, drained and sliced
- 1 bunch fresh basil
- 2 tablespoons of balsamic vinegar (optional)

Directions:

1. Rub the salt and pepper all over the tenderloin.
2. Fill the water bath with water. Set your sous vide machine temperature to 140 °F.
3. Place the pork tenderloin in a food-safe bag and vacuum seal the bag.
4. Place the pork in the water bath, and cook sous vide for 3 hours.
5. Remove the pork tenderloin from the bag and pat dry with a paper towel.
6. Heat the oil in a large skillet over high heat. Sear the tenderloin in the skillet for 45–60 seconds per side. Slice the pork into 1/2" medallions.
7. Assemble the canapés by layering each baguette slice with a slice of pork tenderloin, tomato, bocconcini, and a fresh basil leaf. If desired, drizzle with a little balsamic vinegar.

Nutrition:

- Calories: 564
- Fat: 36 g
- Protein: 19 g

104. GREEN BEAN ALMANDINE

Preparation Time: 8 minutes

Cooking Time: 60 minutes

Serving: 4

Ingredients:

- 3–4 cups of trimmed fresh green beans
- 2 tablespoons of olive oil
- 1 tablespoon of lemon zest
- 2 tablespoons of lemon juice
- 1 teaspoon of sea salt
- 1/2 cup of roughly chopped toasted almonds

Directions:

1. Fill the water bath with water. Set your sous vide machine temperature to 183°F.
2. Place the green beans, oil, and lemon zest in a food-safe bag and vacuum seal the bag. Make sure the beans are lined up side by side and not stacked or piled. Use multiple bags if necessary.
3. Place the beans in the water bath, and cook sous vide for 45–60 minutes.
4. Remove the green beans from the bag and place them on a serving plate. Drizzle with lemon juice and sprinkle with salt.
5. Top with chopped almonds and serve.

Nutrition:

- Calories: 294
- Fat: 20 g
- Protein: 13 g

105. HONEY GINGER CARROTS

Preparation Time: 13 minutes

Cooking Time: 90 minutes

Serving: 4

Ingredients:

- 1-pound of whole baby carrots, peeled
- 2 tablespoons of butter
- 2 tablespoons of honey
- 2 teaspoons of grated fresh ginger root
- 1 teaspoon of sea salt

Directions:

1. Fill the water bath with water. Set your sous vide machine temperature to 183°F.
2. Place the carrots, butter, honey, and ginger in a food-safe bag and vacuum seal the bag. Make sure the carrots are lined up side by side and not stacked or piled. Use multiple bags if necessary.
3. Place the carrots in the water bath, and cook sous vide for 60–90 minutes.
4. Remove the carrots from the bag and place them on a serving plate. Sprinkle with sea salt and serve.

Nutrition:

- Calories: 389
- Fat: 31 g
- Protein: 22 g

106. MASHED POTATOES

Preparation Time: 19 minutes

Cooking Time: 2 hours

Serving: 4

Ingredients:

- 2 pounds of potatoes (white, Yukon Gold, or other), peeled and cut into 1" chunks
- 1/4 cup of butter
- 1/4 cup of heavy cream
- 1/2 cup of whole milk
- 1/2 teaspoon of sea salt
- 1/2 teaspoon of freshly ground black pepper

Directions:

1. Fill the water bath with water. Set your sous vide machine temperature to 183°F.
2. Place the chopped potatoes and butter in a food-safe bag and vacuum seal the bag. Make sure the potatoes are lined up side by side and not stacked or piled. Use multiple bags if necessary.
3. Place the potatoes in the water bath, and cook sous vide for 1 1/2–2 hours.
4. Drain the potatoes in a large bowl. Add the heavy cream, milk, salt, and pepper. Mash the potatoes with a potato masher or a hand blender.

Nutrition:

- Calories: 494
- Fat: 29 g
- Protein: 13 g

107. MAPLE BUTTERNUT SQUASH PURÉE

Preparation Time: 9 minutes

Cooking Time: 3 hours

Serving: 4

Ingredients:

- 1 medium butternut squash
- 1/3 cup of maple syrup
- 1/4 cup of butter
- 1/2 teaspoon of sea salt

Directions:

1. Cut the squash into quarters. Scoop out all the seeds from the inner part of the squash and discard. Peel or cut off the outer skin and discard. Slice the squash flesh into 1" chunks.
2. Fill the water bath with water. Set your sous vide machine temperature to 183 °F.
3. Place the squash chunks, maple syrup, butter, and salt in a large food-safe bag and vacuum seal the bag. Make sure that the squash is in a single layer and not stacked. Use multiple bags if necessary.
4. Place the bag in the water bath, and cook sous vide for 3 hours.
5. Remove the bag from the water bath and let it cool slightly. Pour the squash and any liquid into a food processor or blender and purée until smooth.

Nutrition:

- Calories: 414
- Fat: 29 g
- Protein: 10 g

108. LEEK AND CAULIFLOWER PURÉE

Preparation Time: 13 minutes

Cooking Time: 3 hours

Serving: 4

Ingredients:

- 2 tablespoons of butter
- 2/3 cup of sliced leeks
- 1 medium of head cauliflower
- 2/3 cup of heavy cream
- 1/2 teaspoon of sea salt

Directions:

1. In a small saucepan, melt the butter over medium heat. Add the leeks and cook until soft, about 5 minutes. Cool to room temperature.
2. Fill the water bath with water. Set your sous vide machine temperature to 183°F.
3. Cut the cauliflower into 1/2" slices.
4. Place the cauliflower in a large food-safe bag and vacuum seal the bag. Make sure the cauliflower is placed side by side and not stacked. Use multiple bags if necessary.
5. Place the bag in the water bath, and cook sous vide for 2–3 hours.
6. Remove the bag from the water bath and let it cool slightly. Place the cauliflower, leeks, heavy cream, and salt into a food processor or blender and purée until smooth.

Nutrition:

- Calories: 398
- Fat: 34 g
- Protein: 21 g

109. SZECHUAN BROCCOLI

Preparation Time: 19 minutes
Cooking Time: 2 hours
Serving: 4
Ingredients:

- 3 cups of small broccoli florets
- 2 tablespoons of olive oil
- 3 cloves garlic, minced
- 1 teaspoon of grated fresh ginger root
- 3 tablespoons of soy sauce
- 2 tablespoons of rice vinegar
- 2 tablespoons of granulated sugar
- 2 tablespoons of ketchup
- 1/2 teaspoon of dried red pepper flakes
- 2 tablespoons of toasted sesame seeds

Directions:

1. Fill the water bath with water. Set your sous vide machine temperature to 183 °F.
2. Place the broccoli in a large food-safe bag and vacuum seal the bag. Make sure the broccoli is placed side by side and not stacked. Use multiple bags if necessary.
3. Place the bag in the water bath, and cook sous vide for 1 – 1 1/2 hours.
4. Heat the oil in a medium saucepan over medium heat. Add the garlic and ginger and cook for 2–3 minutes. Add the soy sauce, rice vinegar, sugar, ketchup, and red pepper flakes. Let the sauce simmer for 7–9 minutes. It should thicken slightly.
5. Remove the bag from the water bath. Place the broccoli in a medium bowl and toss with the Szechuan sauce and toasted sesame seeds.

Nutrition:

- Calories: 414
- Fat: 36 g
- Protein: 19 g

110. BUTTERED CORN ON THE COB

Preparation Time: 14 minutes

Cooking Time: 3 hours

Serving: 4

Ingredients:

- 4 cobs of corn, shucked and cleaned
- 2 tablespoons of butter
- 1 teaspoon of sea salt

Directions:

1. Fill the water bath with water. Set your sous vide machine temperature to 183°F.
2. Place the corn and butter in a food-safe bag and vacuum seal the bag. Make sure the cobs are lined up side by side and not stacked or piled. Use multiple bags if necessary.
3. Place the corn in the water bath, and cook sous vide for 1 1/2–3 hours.
4. Remove the corn from the bag. Sprinkle with sea salt and serve.

Nutrition:

- Calories: 294
- Fat: 21 g
- Protein: 13 g

111. RATATOUILLE

Preparation Time: 11 minutes
Cooking Time: 3 hours
Serving: 4
Ingredients:

- 2 tablespoons of olive oil
- 1 medium sweet onion, diced
- 1 medium green bell pepper, cored and diced
- 2 cloves of garlic, minced
- 2 cups of peeled and cubed eggplant, no larger than ½" pieces
- 2 cups of cubed zucchini, no larger than ½" pieces
- 2 medium tomatoes, diced
- 1 teaspoon of sea salt
- 1 teaspoon of dried marjoram or tarragon
- 1/2 teaspoon of freshly ground black pepper

Directions:

1. In a medium skillet, heat the oil over medium heat. Add the onion, pepper, and garlic. Cook until the onions are transparent and the peppers are soft about 5–7 minutes. Cool to room temperature.
2. Fill the water bath with water. Set your sous vide machine temperature to 183 °F.
3. In a large bowl, toss together the sautéed onion and pepper with all the remaining ingredients. Dump the mixture into a food-safe bag and vacuum seal the bag. Make sure the ratatouille is an even thickness within the bag, about 1 – 1 1/2" thick. Use multiple bags if necessary.
4. Place the bag in the water bath, and cook sous vide for 3 hours.
5. Remove from the water bath and serve hot.

Nutrition:

- Calories: 411
- Fat: 34 g
- Protein: 23 g

112. SOUS-VIDE MASHED POTATOES

Preparation Time: 11 minutes

Cooking Time: 90 minutes

Serving: 2

Ingredients:

- 500 g of potatoes
- 120 ml of milk
- 100 g of butter
- 1 teaspoon of nutmeg
- 1 sprig of rosemary
- 3 cloves of garlic

Directions:

1. Preheat the Sous-vide water bath to 90 ° C.
2. Peel the potatoes and cut them into 3 mm thick slices.
3. Vacuum the potatoes with the peeled garlic cloves, rosemary, milk, and butter in a suitable bag.
4. Let the potatoes cook in a water bath for 90 minutes.
5. Remove the bag and let the butter sauce drain through a sieve, but collect it. Collect the sprig of rosemary and garlic.
6. Mash the potatoes and gradually add the butter sauce to the desired consistency. Season to taste with pepper, salt, and nutmeg.

Nutrition:

- Calories: 374
- Fat: 27 g
- Protein: 19 g

113. A BED OF VEGETABLES SOUS VIDE

Preparation Time: 9 minutes

Cooking Time: 48 minutes

Serving: 4

Ingredients:

- 1 cucumber
- 3 carrots
- 1 sweet potato
- 1 red, green, and yellow pepper each
- 1 leek
- 1 pinch each of chili powder, salt, and pepper
- 1 tablespoon of olive oil

Directions:

1. Clean all vegetables, peel them if necessary, and cut them into bite-sized pieces. Marinate in a bowl with the oil, chili, pepper, and salt.
2. Vacuum seal in a suitable bag.
3. Preheat the water bath to 85 °C and let the vegetables cook for 40 minutes. This also works in the steamer.
4. Once removed from the bag, the vegetables are ready to be served on the plate.
5. Drape meat or fish on top and let the vegetables turn into a bed.

Nutrition:

- Calories: 398
- Fat: 26 g
- Protein: 19 g

114. SAUERKRAUT

Preparation Time: 9 minutes

Cooking Time: 46 minutes

Serving: 4

Ingredients:

- 500 g of sauerkraut
- 2 red onions
- 2 tablespoons of butter
- 1 teaspoon of sugar
- 2 tablespoons of apple cider vinegar
- 2 bay leaves
- Juniper berries
- diced bacon and apple (Optional)

Directions:

1. Preheat the water bath to 90 °C.
2. Sweat the onions cut into small pieces in butter and let them cool again.
3. Sauerkraut, if you like diced apples, onions, vinegar, sugar, and spices, put them in a Sous-vide bag and close under vacuum.
4. Cook for 45 minutes in a water bath.
5. Remove from the bag and season to taste. Serve as a side dish with delicious sous-vide meat or fish.
6. The recipe can also be modified regionally.

Nutrition:

- Calories: 294
- Fat: 21 g
- Protein: 10 g

115. ASPARAGUS

Preparation Time: 11 minutes

Cooking Time: 24 minutes

Serving: 4

Ingredients:

- 500 g of white asparagus
- 30 g of butter
- Zest of one lemon
- ½ teaspoon of each of sugar and salt

Directions:

1. Peel the asparagus, cut off the woody end.
2. Put the asparagus in the vacuum bag and vacuum seal together with the lemon zest, butter, salt, and sugar.
3. Preheat the water bath to 85 °C and add the asparagus for 30 minutes. This also works with the steamer.
4. When you open the bag, the buttery asparagus is ready.
5. A hollandaise sauce with boiled potatoes goes well with it.

Nutrition:

- Calories: 313
- Fat: 26 g
- Protein: 13 g

116. HOLLANDAISE SAUCE

Preparation Time: minutes

Cooking Time: 30 minutes

Serving: 4

Ingredients:

- 3 egg yolks
- 4 tablespoons of white wine or water
- 150 g of butter
- Juice of ½ lemon
- 1 pinch each of pepper and salt

Directions:

1. Beat the egg yolks with the whisk over steam until frothy.
2. Add the butter gradually in flakes and stir.
3. Add lemon juice and keep stirring. Season to taste with salt and pepper and whisk until the sauce becomes creamy
4. The sauce goes well with asparagus, fish, vegetables, or seafood.

Nutrition:

- Calories: 314
- Fat: 29 g
- Protein: 14 g

117. ROSEMARY POTATOES

Preparation Time: 9 minutes

Cooking Time: 55 minutes

Serving: 2

Ingredients:

- 500 g of potatoes
- 1 tablespoon of olive oil
- 2 cloves of garlic
- 1 bay leaf
- 1 sprig of rosemary
- 1 level teaspoon of salt

Directions:

1. Peel the potato and cut it into smaller cubes.
2. Put the olive oil, salt, bay leaf, peeled garlic cloves, and rosemary in a Sous-vide bag and seal it airtight with a vacuum.
3. Preheat the water bath to 85 °C and cook the potatoes for 40 minutes. The cooking time also depends on the size of the potato cubes.
4. After the potatoes have been removed from the bag, they can be browned briefly in the pan until they are golden.

Nutrition:

- Calories: 269
- Fat: 26 g
- Protein: 14 g

118. HOKKAIDO PUMPKIN

Preparation Time: 11 minutes

Cooking Time: 16 minutes

Serving: 2

Ingredients:

- 400 g of pumpkin meat from Hokkaido
- 1 tablespoon of butter
- Some grated ginger
- 1 tablespoon of apple juice
- 1 pinch of salt and pepper each

Directions:

1. Cut up the washed pumpkin. Scrape out the seeds with a spoon (these can still be used for other purposes).
2. Cut the Hokkaido with the peel into bite-sized pieces and vacuum seal in a suitable bag with the apple juice, pepper, salt, 1 teaspoon of butter, and ginger.
3. Preheat the water bath to 80 °C and cook the pumpkin for 20 minutes using the sous-vide method or a steam oven.
4. After removing the pumpkin cubes, fry them briefly in hot butter.

Nutrition:

- Calories: 399
- Fat: 31 g
- Protein: 15 g

119. NAPKIN DUMPLINGS

Preparation Time: 12 minutes
Cooking Time: 75 minutes
Serving: 4
Ingredients:

- 250 g of cubes of dumpling bread
- 250 ml of milk
- ½ teaspoon of salt
- 1 handful of parsley
- 2 tablespoons of butter
- 3 eggs
- Some grated nutmeg

Directions:

1. Put the dumpling bread in a bowl.
2. Sauté the parsley briefly in hot butter and mix with the dumpling bread.
3. Separate eggs. Mix the egg yolks with salt, milk, and a little nutmeg. Mix this mixture with the dumpling bread.
4. Beat the egg whites until stiff and mix carefully with the dumpling bread.
5. Cover and let rest for ½ hour.
6. Preheat the water bath to 82 °C.
7. Knead the mass quickly and shape into two rolls. The length and thickness depend on the sous-vide pot used.
8. Seal the rolls individually or side by side in a suitable bag and cook for 60 minutes.
9. Take the dumpling rolls out of the bath and cut them into slices for serving.

Nutrition:

- Calories: 393
- Fat: 31 g
- Protein: 17 g

120. CARROT STICKS

Preparation Time: 9 minutes

Cooking Time: 61 minutes

Serving: 4

Ingredients:

- 400 g of carrots
- 1 tablespoon of butter
- 1 teaspoon of fennel seeds
- 1 teaspoon of grated ginger

Directions:

1. Peel the washed carrots finely with a potato peeler and cut them into sticks.
2. Place these next to each other in a vacuum bag. Add the fennel seeds, ginger to the bag, and close the bag airtight.
3. Preheat the water bath to 80 °C and cook the carrot sticks for 60 minutes. The whole thing also works in the steamer.
4. In the end, rinse the carrots in the bag with cold, preferably ice, water. Finally, toss the carrots through hot butter in a pan.

Nutrition:

- Calories: 294
- Fat: 21 g
- Protein: 17 g

121. SOUS-VIDE BOLOGNESE SAUCE FOR SPAGHETTI

Preparation Time: 8 minutes
Cooking Time: 3 hours
Serving: 4
Ingredients:

- 250 g of ground beef
- 1 clove of garlic
- 1 onion
- 300 g of tomato puree
- 1 tablespoon of rapeseed oil
- 1 teaspoon of dried basil
- ½ teaspoon of chili flakes
- 1 tablespoon of sugar
- Salt

Directions:

1. Preheat the water bath to 72 °C.
2. Mix tomato puree and minced meat in a bowl with sugar, basil, chili flakes, and 1-teaspoon of salt to form a smooth sauce.
3. Sauté onion cubes and finely chopped garlic clove in hot oil until golden brown. Add to the mince mixture and stir.
4. Divide the sauce between two bags and vacuum seal.
5. Cook for 2 hours and 40 minutes in a water bath.
6. Prepare pasta according to the instructions on the packet.
7. Serve pasta with Bolognese sauce.

Nutrition:

- Calories: 424
- Fat: 29 g
- Protein: 14 g

CHAPTER 12. SOUP AND STEW RECIPES

122. CREAM OF CELERY SOUP

Preparation Time: 18 minutes

Cooking Time: 60 minutes

Serving: 2

Ingredients:

- 2 cups of celery, diced into large pieces
- ½ cup of russet potatoes, peeled, diced into small pieces
- ½ cup of leek, diced into large pieces
- ½ cup of stock (vegetable or chicken)
- ½ cup of heavy cream
- 1 tablespoon of butter
- 1 bay leaf
- 1 teaspoon of kosher salt or to taste
- White pepper powder to taste

Directions:

1. Set your sous vide machine to 180 °F.
2. Place all the ingredients in a ziplock or a vacuum-seal bag. Remove the air by using the water displacement method or a vacuum-sealed. Seal and then submerge in the water bath. Cook for 1 hour or until the vegetables are tender.
3. When done, remove the bay leaf and puree the soup. Strain through a wire mesh strainer and discard the solids. Serve hot.

Nutrition:

- Calories: 372
- Fat: 23 g
- Protein: 14 g

123. CARROT & CORIANDER SOUP

Preparation Time: 13 minutes

Cooking Time: 1 hour 45 minutes

Serving: 4

Ingredients:

- 1 lb. of carrots
- 1 cup of coconut cream
- 2 teaspoons of ground coriander
- 1 teaspoon of ground cumin
- 1 clove of garlic, crushed
- Fresh coriander, chopped, to serve

Directions:

1. Set your sous vide machine to 190 °F.
2. Put carrots, coconut cream, coriander, cumin, and garlic into a ziplock or vacuum-seal bag and remove all the air with the water displacement method or a vacuum-sealed. Seal and submerge the bag in the water bath and cook for 1 hour and 45 minutes.
3. Transfer the ingredients to a blender, breaking up the carrots as you remove them, and blend until smooth.
4. Serve warm, topping with chopped coriander to taste.

Nutrition:

- Calories: 260
- Fat: 27 g
- Protein: 12 g

124. SPRING ONION SOUP

Preparation Time: 14 minutes

Cooking Time: 60 minutes

Serving: 2

Ingredients:

- 2 bunches of spring onions, rinsed, trimmed, chopped
- 4 cloves of garlic, peeled, chopped
- 1 large russet potato, peeled, diced
- 2 teaspoons of olive oil plus extra for serving
- 2 teaspoons of soy sauce
- Salt to taste
- Pepper powder to taste
- 2-3 tablespoons of fresh parsley leaves for garnishing

Directions:

1. Set your sous vide machine to 180 °F.
2. Add all the ingredients to a zip lock or a vacuum-seal bag and remove all the air with the water displacement method or a vacuum-sealed. Seal and submerge the bag in the water bath and cook for 45 minutes to 1 hour.
3. Remove the pouch and transfer into a blender, and blend until smooth and creamy.
4. Ladle into individual soup bowls. Garnish with parsley and serve.

Nutrition:

- Calories: 368
- Fat: 28 g
- Protein: 10 g

125. CHICKEN & VEGETABLE SOUP

Preparation Time: 12 minutes
Cooking Time: 68 minutes
Serving: 2
Ingredients:

- 1/2 cup of zucchini, diced
- 1/2 cup of red bell pepper, diced
- 1/2 cup of cauliflower, chopped
- 3 baby carrots, chopped
- 1 medium onion, chopped
- 2 cups of fresh spinach leaves
- 1/2 teaspoon of garlic powder or to taste
- 1/2 teaspoon of onion powder
- Sea salt to taste
- Black pepper powder to taste
- Cayenne pepper to taste
- 1 cup of chicken, diced, sous vide cooked
- ½ tablespoon of olive oil
- 2 cups of chicken broth

Directions:

1. Set your sous vide machine to 180 °F.
2. Place all the vegetables and spices in a bowl. Mix well and place it into a zip lock or a vacuum-seal bag. Remove all the air with the water displacement method or vacuum-sealed. Seal and submerge the bag in the water bath and cook for 1 hour or until the vegetables are tender.
3. To make the soup, heat olive oil in a soup pot over medium heat. Add broth and bring to a boil.
4. Lower heat and add chicken and cooked vegetables along with their juices. Simmer for 5-7 minutes.
5. Serve hot.

Nutrition:

- Calories: 369
- Fat: 26 g
- Protein: 14 g

126. CAULIFLOWER SOUP

Preparation Time: 9 minutes
Cooking Time: 70 minutes
Serving: 2
Ingredients:
- 1 large head cauliflower, break into florets
- 2 shallots, chopped
- 4 cups of vegetable stock
- ½ cup of white wine
- 1 ½ cup of sour cream
- Juice of a lemon
- 1 teaspoon of Ras el Hanout
- Zest of 2 lemons, grated
- A few slices of roasted caraway bread
- 1 teaspoon of ground cumin
- Cooking spray
- 1 cup of grated cauliflower to serve
- Extra virgin olive oil to serve

Directions:
1. Place a skillet over medium heat. Spray with cooking spray. Add the shallots and sauté for a couple of minutes.
2. Set your sous vide machine to 167 °F. Place the shallots, cauliflower, stock, wine, sour cream, cream, and lemon juice into a ziplock or a vacuum-seal bag and remove all the air with the water displacement method vacuum-sealed. Seal and submerge the bag in the water bath.
3. Meanwhile, mix the grated cauliflower, Ras el Hanout and half of the lemon zest.
4. Remove the pouch from the cooker, transfer it into the blender, and blend until smooth. Season with salt and pepper. Pulse a couple of times to mix well.
5. Place the grated cauliflower mixture on bread slices. Drizzle some oil over it. Sprinkle salt, cumin, and the remaining lemon zest.
6. Ladle into individual soup bowls. Serve with the garnished bread slices.

Nutrition:
- Calories: 370
- Fat: 22 g
- Protein: 14 g

127. BUTTERNUT SQUASH & APPLE SOUP

Preparation Time: 12 minutes

Cooking Time: 60 minutes

Serving: 2

Ingredients:

- 1 small butternut squash, peeled, sliced
- 1 medium apple like Granny Smith, peeled, cored, sliced
- 3 green onions, trimmed, sliced
- 1/2 teaspoon of sea salt or to taste.
- 1/2 cup of light cream

Directions:

1. Set your sous vide machine to 185 °F.
2. Place all the vegetables and apples into a ziplock or a vacuum-seal bag and remove all the air with the water displacement method or a vacuum-sealed. Seal and submerge the bag in the water bath, cook for 2 hours or until the vegetables are cooked through.
3. When done, puree the soup. Add salt and cream and blend again. Serve hot.

Nutritions:

- Calories: 372
- Fat: 26 g
- Protein: 11 g

128. CHICKEN NOODLE SOUP

Preparation Time: 13 minutes
Cooking Time: 60 minutes
Serving: 2
Ingredients:
- 3 pounds of whole chicken, trussed
- 3 cups of carrots, finely diced
- 9 cups of chicken stock
- 3 cups of white onion, finely diced
- 3 cups of celery, finely diced
- Salt to taste
- Pepper to taste
- 2 bay leaves
- 1 ½ pound of dried egg noodles

Directions:
1. Set your sous vide machine to 150 °F.
2. Add all the ingredients except noodles into a large zip lock bag or a vacuum-seal bag. Remove all the air with the water displacement method or vacuum-sealed. Seal and submerge the bag in the water bath and cook for 6 hours or until the vegetables and chicken are cooked. Cover the cooker with plastic wrap so that the evaporation is kept to the minimum.
3. When done, remove it from the cooker. Transfer into a large pot. Place the pot over medium heat.
4. Cook for around 20 minutes. Remove the chicken with a slotted spoon.
5. Add noodles and cook until al dente. Shred the chicken with a pair of forks and add it back into the pot.
6. Heat thoroughly and serve.

Nutrition:
- Calories: 366
- Fat: 29 g
- Protein: 15 g

129. BORSCHT

Preparation Time: 9 minutes
Cooking Time: 60 minutes
Serving: 4
Ingredients:
- 2 large beets, peeled and sliced
- 2 large carrots, peeled and sliced
- ½ large onion, peeled and sliced
- 1 small potato, peeled and sliced
- ¼ head red cabbage, thinly sliced
- 2 quarts of stock of your choice
- ½ cup of chopped fresh dill
- 3 tablespoons of red wine vinegar
- Salt and pepper to taste
- Sour cream, to serve
- Fresh dill, to serve

Directions:
1. Set your sous vide machine to 182 °F.
2. Put the beets, carrots, and onions into a ziplock or a vacuum-seal bag and remove all the air with the water displacement method or a vacuum-sealed. Do the same with the cabbage in a separate pouch.
3. Place the bags in the sous vide cooker for at least 1 hour. They can stay in for up to
4. Remove the vegetables. Puree the beets, carrots, and onions. Leave the cabbage to the side.
5. Bring the stock to the boil, adding the pureed vegetables, cabbage, dill, vinegar, salt, and pepper. Let the soup simmer until you are ready to eat.
6. Serve the soup with a spoonful of sour cream and some fresh dill.

Nutrition:
- Calories: 384
- Fat: 28 g
- Protein: 11 g

130. CREAMY TOMATO SOUP

Preparation Time: 18 minutes
Cooking Time: 60 minutes
Serving: 2
Ingredients:

- ¼ cup of butter
- 3 tablespoons of flour
- 2 ¼ cups of milk
- ½ cup of heavy cream
- 1 ½ can of whole or diced tomatoes, peeled
- 1 fresh tomato, chopped
- 1 small green pepper, chopped
- 1 clove garlic, chopped
- 1 tablespoon of dried basil leaves
- A pinch of cayenne pepper
- Tabasco sauce to taste
- ½ teaspoon of salt or to taste
- ½ teaspoon of black pepper powder or to taste
- 2 Onions, quartered

Directions:
1. Place a saucepan over medium heat. Add half the butter. When the butter starts melting, add flour and sauté for a couple of minutes, stirring constantly.
2. Slowly add milk and continue stirring until the mixture thickens.
3. Add cream and continue stirring. Do not boil. Remove from heat and keep aside.
4. Place another saucepan over medium heat. Add the remaining butter. When butter melts, add onions, garlic, and green pepper and sauté until the onions are translucent. Add tomatoes and basil and simmer for a few minutes.
5. Lower heat and add the white sauce, cayenne pepper, Tabasco, salt, and pepper.
6. Set your sous vide machine to 172-175 °F.
7. Place all the vegetables into a ziplock or a vacuum-seal bag and remove all the air with the water displacement method or a vacuum-sealed. Seal and submerge the bag in the water bath cook for 45 minutes.
8. When done, puree the soup. Serve hot.

Nutrition:

- Calories: 362
- Fat: 26 g
- Protein: 12 g

131. CHILLED PEA & CUCUMBER SOUP

Preparation Time: 9 minutes

Cooking Time: 75 minutes

Serving: 4

Ingredients:

- 10 oz. of peas
- 1 onion, diced
- 1 clove of garlic, crushed
- 2 Lebanese cucumbers, seeded, roughly chopped
- ¼ cup of mint leaves
- 2 cups of vegetable stock, chilled

Directions:

1. Set your sous vide machine to 180 °F.
2. Put the peas, onion, and garlic into a large ziplock or vacuum-seal bag. Seal the bag using the water displacement method or vacuum-sealed.
3. Cook peas for 1 hour. When done, submerge in an ice bath for 15 minutes.
4. Puree the contents of the bag with the cucumber and mint.
5. Slowly add the stock until ingredients are well combined and you reach a smooth consistency.
6. Serve chilled, stirring the soup if there is any separation.

Nutrition:

- Calories: 381
- Fat: 30 g
- Protein: 22 g

132. SLOW CHICKEN STOCK

Preparation Time: 11 minutes
Cooking Time: 71 minutes
Serving: 12
Ingredients:
- 2 pounds of chicken bones
- 2 cups of diced carrots
- 2 cups of diced celery
- 2 cups of diced leeks
- 2 tablespoons of extra virgin olive oil
- 8 cups of water
- 1 tablespoon of whole black peppercorns
- 2 bay leaves

Directions:
1. Set your sous vide machine to 180 °F and preheat your oven to 450 °F.
2. In a large bowl, mix the chicken bones, carrots, celery, and leeks with olive oil. Place the ingredients onto a sheet pan and roast until golden brown, about 20 minutes.
3. Transfer all of the bones and vegetables, along with any accumulated juices and brown bits on the sheet pan, into a large ziplock or vacuum-seal bag. Add the water, peppercorns, and bay leaves. Seal the bag using the water displacement method or vacuum-sealed.
4. Submerge the bag in the water bath and set the timer for 12 hours. Cover the water bath with plastic wrap to minimize water evaporation. Continuously top off the pot with more water to keep the bag fully submerged underwater.
5. When ready, strain the ingredients and then portion out the stock into airtight containers. Store in the refrigerator for up to 1 week or freeze up to 2 months.

Nutrition:
- Calories: 379
- Fat: 21 g
- Protein: 16 g

133. SOUS VIDE CORNISH HEN SOUP

Preparation Time: 13 minutes
Cooking Time: 62 minutes
Serving: 4
Ingredients:
- 2 tablespoons of coconut oil
- 4 medium shallots, smashed and peeled
- 3 cloves of garlic, smashed and peeled
- 2 lemongrass stalks, roughly chopped
- piece of fresh ginger, thinly sliced
- 5 dried red Thai chilies
- 2 teaspoons of dried green peppercorns, coarsely ground
- 1 teaspoon of ground turmeric cups water
- 2 whole Cornish game hens
- 1/2 cup of chopped cilantro
- 2 scallions, coarsely chopped
- 2 tablespoons of Asian fish sauce
- 1 teaspoon of finely grated lime zest
- Kosher salt and freshly ground black pepper

Directions:
1. Set your sous vide machine to 150 °F.
2. In a large skillet, melt the coconut oil over medium heat. When hot, add the shallots, garlic, lemongrass, ginger, chilies, peppercorns, and turmeric. Cook, occasionally stirring until shallots begin to soften, about 5 minutes.
3. Add the water to the skillet and stir, making sure to scrape the bottom of the pan. Carefully transfer to a large ziplock or vacuum-seal bag. Add the game hens to the bag and then seal using the water displacement method. Place the bag in the water bath and set the timer for 4 hours.
4. When ready, remove the bag from the water bath and take out the hens. Let the hen rest until cool enough to handle. Separate the legs, wings, and breast meat.
5. Add the cooking liquid to a large pot and bring it to a simmer over medium-high heat. Stir in the cilantro, scallions, fish sauce, lime juice, and game hen meat. Season to taste with salt and pepper.

Nutrition:
- Calories: 370
- Fat: 22 g
- Protein: 14 g

134. CHICKEN CURRY SOUP

Preparation Time: 16 minutes
Cooking Time: 70 minutes
Serving: 8
Ingredients:
- 1 (4-pounds of whole chicken, trussed)
- 6 cups of water
- 2 cups of diced carrots
- 2 cups of diced celery
- 2 cups of diced white onion
- Kosher salt and freshly ground black pepper
- 1 tablespoon of coconut oil
- 1 cup of thinly sliced shallots
- 2 tablespoons of red curry paste
- 1 tablespoon of curry powder
- 2 garlic of cloves, minced
- 1 teaspoon of ground turmeric
- 1 teaspoon of ground coriander
- 1 teaspoon of sugar
- 1/2 teaspoon of crushed red pepper
- 4 cups of fresh spinach leaves
- 1/4 cup of thinly sliced scallions
- 1 tablespoon of fish sauce
- Cilantro and lime wedges, for serving

Directions:
1. Set your sous vide machine to 150 °F.
2. In a large ziplock or vacuum-seal bag, combine the chicken, water, carrots, celery, and onion. Season with salt and pepper. Seal the bag by using the water displacement technique or a vacuum seal. Set a timer for 6 hours. Cover the water bath with plastic wrap to minimize water evaporation. Continuously top up the pot of water to keep the chicken fully submerged.
3. When the timer goes off, remove the bag from the water bath. Remove the chicken from the bag and then strain the soup with a fine mesh strainer. Discard the rest of the vegetables.
4. Let the chicken rest until cool to the touch, then remove and shred the meat.
5. Heat the coconut oil in a stockpot or Dutch oven over medium heat. Add the shallots and cook until softened.
6. Stir in the curry paste, curry powder, garlic, turmeric, coriander, sugar, and crushed red pepper. Continue to cook for 5 minutes, and then add in the reserved chicken cooking liquid and bring to a simmer. Continue to simmer for 30 minutes to allow the flavors to meld.

7. Near the end of the cooking process, add the spinach, scallions, fish sauce, and shredded chicken. Simmer until heated through, and the spinach has wilted for about 2 minutes. Season to taste with salt and pepper. Serve topped with cilantro and lime wedges.

Nutrition:
- Calories: 379
- Fat: 34 g
- Protein: 15 g

135. STRACCIATELLA ALLA ROMANA SOUP

Preparation Time: 11 minutes
Cooking Time: 63 minutes
Serving: 8
Ingredients:

- 1 (4-pounds of whole chicken, trussed
- 6 cups of water
- 2 cups of diced carrots
- 2 cups of diced celery
- 2 cups of diced white onion
- Kosher salt and freshly ground black pepper
- 1/2 cup of grated Parmesan cheese
- 4 large eggs, beaten
- 1/4 cup of thinly sliced scallion
- 2 tablespoons of freshly squeezed lemon juice
- 2 tablespoons of minced fresh parsley
- 2 cups of baby spinach

Directions:

1. Set your sous vide machine to 150 °F.
2. In a ziplock or vacuum-seal bag, combine the chicken, water, carrots, celery, and onion. Season with salt and pepper. Seal the bag using the water displacement technique and then place the bag into the hot water bath. Set a timer for 6 hours. Cover the water bath with plastic wrap to minimize water evaporation. Continuously top off the pot with water to keep the chicken fully submerged.
3. When the timer goes off, remove the bag from the water bath and carefully remove the chicken from the bag. Strain the cooking liquid through a fine-mesh strainer into a stockpot. Discard the rest of the ingredients.
4. Let the chicken rest for about 20 minutes or until cool to the touch. Remove and shred the meat.
5. Bring the cooking liquid to a simmer over medium-high heat.
6. In a medium bowl, whisk together the Parmesan, eggs, scallion, lemon juice, and parsley. While stirring the stock, slowly pour in the egg mixture in a thin ribbon. Let the eggs cook undisturbed for 1 minute, and then stir.
7. Add the spinach and shredded chicken and simmer until heated through and the spinach has wilted. Season & serve.

Nutrition:

- Calories: 391
- Fat: 36 g
- Protein: 14 g

136. OYSTER STEW

Preparation Time: 9 minutes
Cooking Time: 62 minutes
Serving: 4
Ingredients:
- 4 tablespoons of unsalted butter
- 1 cup of thinly sliced leeks
- 1 small garlic clove, minced
- 2 cups of shucked oysters with liquid
- 2 cups of whole milk
- 2 cups of heavy cream
- 1 bay leaf
- Kosher salt and freshly ground black pepper

Directions:
1. Set your sous vide machine to 120°F.
2. Melt the butter in a large skillet over medium heat and then add the leeks and garlic. Sauté while stirring until the vegetables are tender. Set aside to cool.
3. In a large ziplock or vacuum-seal bag, combine the oysters, milk, cream, bay leaf, and leek mixture. Seal the bag using the water displacement method or a vacuum-sealed and then place it in the water bath. Set the timer for 1 hour.
4. When the timer goes off, remove the bag from the water bath. Divide the stew into bowls and remove the bay leaf. Season with salt and pepper to taste and serve.

Nutrition:
- Calories: 376
- Fat: 26 g
- Protein: 12 g

137. CHICKEN STOCK

Preparation Time: 18 minutes
Cooking Time: 8 hours
Serving: 8
Ingredients:

- 10 lbs. of chicken bones
- 1 lb. of yellow onion peeled and cut in half
- 8 oz. of carrots, chopped
- 8 oz. of celery, chopped
- ½ teaspoon of black peppercorn
- 10 sprigs of fresh thyme
- Small handful parsley stem
- 1-piece of bay leaf

Directions:

1. Roast your chicken bones for about 1 ½ hour at 400 °F in your oven.
2. Add the roasted chicken bones, onion, and the rest of the ingredients to a resealable zipper bag.
3. Add the water (reserve 1 cup and seal using the immersion method.
4. Prepare the water bath to a temperature of 194 °F using your immersion circulator
5. Submerge underwater and cook for 6-8 hours.
6. Strain the mixture from the zip bag through a metal mesh into a large-sized bowl
7. Cool the stock using an ice bath and place it in your oven overnight.
8. Scrape the surface and discard fat.
9. Use as needed.

Nutrition:

- Calories: 83
- Protein: 173 g
- Fat: 137 g

138. SPRING MINESTRONE SOUP

Preparation Time: 10 minutes
Cooking Time: 40 minutes
Servings: 4
Ingredients:
- 2 chopped carrots
- 1 sliced leek
- sprigs of thyme
- 3 chopped red potatoes
- 2 tablespoons of olive oil
- 2 cups of vegetable broth
- 1 bunch sliced asparagus
- 2 cups of navy beans
- 2 tablespoons of chopped dill
- ¼ tsp of Salt

Directions:
1. Take a large mixing pan and combine the carrots, thyme, leek, and salt.
2. Set the sous vide machine to 165 °F.
3. Take the above mixture in a ziplock bag and seal it.
4. Place the bag in sous vide and cook for 8 minutes.
5. Take a large skillet and take the cooked vegetables, add red potatoes, vegetable broth and cook for 25 minutes until they turn tender.
6. Then add asparagus and cook for more than 3 minutes. Remove thyme and add navy beans, chopped dill, salt, and pepper.
7. Serve hot.

Nutrition:
- Calories 330
- Protein 7 g
- Fat 7 g

139. MUSHROOM ORZO GREEN SOUP

Preparation Time: 5 minutes
Cooking Time: 35 minutes
Servings: 6
Ingredients:
- 1 cup of sliced mushroom
- 1 cup of orzo
- 3 cups of sliced spinach
- 3 cups of broccoli
- 2 cups of vegetable broth
- 2 tablespoons of olive oil
- 1 1/4 cup of celery
- 1/2 cup of shallots
- 1/4 cup of garlic
- ½ tablespoon of Salt, pepper, and basil pesto

Directions:
1. In a large cooking pan, mix the celery, shallots, garlic, salt, and oil.
2. Set the sous vide machine to 175 °F.
3. Take the above mixture in a ziplock pouch. Seal it under vacuum or underwater.
4. Place the bag in sous vide and cook for 8 minutes.
5. Take the cooked vegetables in a skillet and add vegetable broth and broccoli. Simmer for 15 minutes.
6. Add the mushroom, orzo, spinach, and simmer again for 10 minutes until all vegetables soften.
7. Sprinkle salt, pepper, basil pesto, and serve hot.

Nutrition:
- Calories: 230
- Protein: 7 g
- Fat: 8 g

140. SQUASH AND LENTIL STEW

Preparation Time: 15 minutes
Cooking Time: 35 minutes
Servings: 6
Ingredients:

- 1 pound of green lentils
- 2 sliced shallots
- 1 butternut squash
- 2 cups of baby spinach
- 2 cups of vegetable broth
- 1 tablespoon of chopped ginger
- 1 teaspoon of coriander powder
- 1/2 teaspoon of cardamom powder
- 1 tablespoon of vinegar
- ¼ tsp of Salt and pepper
- ½ cup of vegetable oil

Directions:

1. Take the squash and peel it. Cut it into 1 1/2" pieces.
2. Set the sous vide machine to 165 °F.
3. Take the lentils, squash in the sous vide bag.
4. Place the bag in sous vide and cook for 5 minutes.
5. Transfer it to a cooking pan. Add shallot, ginger, oil, cardamom powder, coriander powder, salt, and vegetable broth.
6. Cook on high flame for 12 minutes.
7. Add spinach, vinegar, salt, pepper, and serve hot.

Nutrition:

- Calories: 325
- Protein: 19 g
- Fat: 4 g

CHAPTER 13.   DESSERT RECIPES

141.   BUTTERED SPICED APPLES

Preparation Time: 21 minutes
Cooking Time: 2 hours
Serving: 6
Ingredients:
- Zest and juice from 1 lemon
- 6 small apples
- 6 tablespoons of unsalted butter
- 1/2 teaspoon of salt
- 1/2 teaspoon of ground cinnamon
- 1/4 teaspoon of ground nutmeg
- 1 heaping teaspoon of dark brown sugar
- 1 heaping tablespoon of dark or golden raisins

Directions:
1. Preheat your Anova Precision Cooker to 170 °F or 77 °C. Peel and core the apples, soften the butter, and completely zest the lemon.
2. Coat the apples with lemon juice. Place the lemon zest in a bowl and combine with the cinnamon, sugar, nutmeg, raisins, butter, and salt. Place an equal amount of the mixture in the hollowed-out center of each apple.
3. Put 2 apples in each bag and set your Anova timer for 2 hours.
4. Remove apples from the bag and serve immediately with cooking liquid.

Nutrition:
- Calories: 229
- Fat: 12 g
- Protein 0.9 g

142. STRAWBERRIES

Preparation Time: 11 minutes

Cooking Time: 16 minutes

Serving: 4

Ingredients:

- 12 oz. of strawberries trimmed
- 2 tablespoons of champagne
- 2 teaspoon of sugar

Directions:

1. Preheat your Anova Precision Cooker to 185 °F or 85 °C.
2. Place all the ingredients in a sous vide bag and place the bag in the preheated container, and set your Anova timer for 15 minutes.
3. Meanwhile, prepare an ice bath. When the strawberries are cooked, put them directly in the ice bath until they're cold.

Nutrition:

- Calories: 80
- Fat: 12 g
- Protein 0.6 g

143. RED WINE POACHED PEARS

Preparation Time: 9 minutes
Cooking Time: 360 minutes
Serving: 4
Ingredients:
- 4 ripe Bosc pears
- 1 cup of red wine
- 1/2 cup of granulated sugar
- 1/4 cup of sweet vermouth
- 1 teaspoon of salt
- 3 (3-inch pieces) of orange zest
- 1 vanilla bean
- vanilla ice cream

Directions:
1. Preheat your Anova Precision Cooker to 175 °F or 79 °C. Peel the pear and scrape the vanilla bean seeds.
2. Put everything except for the ice cream in a sous vide bag. Then, place the bag in the preheated container and set your Anova timer for 1 hour.
3. When the pears are cooked, slice them up and core them. Reserve the juices from the bag.
4. Place the sliced pears in 4 bowls and add a scoop of ice cream. Top with the reserved juices and serve.

Nutrition:
- Calories: 299
- Fat: 0.3 g
- Protein 1 g

144. ROSE WATER APRICOTS

Preparation Time: 11 minutes

Cooking Time: 60 minutes

Serving: 8

Ingredients:

- 8 apricots
- 1 teaspoon of rosewater
- 1/2 cup of water

Directions:

1. Preheat your Anova Precision Cooker to 180 °F or 82 °C. Cut the apricots in half and remove the pit.
2. Place all the ingredients in a sous vide bag. Then, place the bag in your preheated container and set your Anova timer for 1 hour.
3. When the peaches are cooked, serve in a small bowl or plate.

Nutrition:

- Calories: 17
- Fat: 0.2 g
- Protein 0.5 g

145. DOLCE DE LECHE

Preparation Time: 6 minutes

Cooking Time: 13 hours

Serving: 8

Ingredients:

- 12 oz. of sweetened condensed milk

Directions:

1. Preheat your Anova Precision Cooker to 185 °F or 85 °C.
2. Put the milk in a sous vide bag or a pint-size mason jar.
3. Put the bag or Mason jar in your preheated container and set your Anova timer for 13 hours.
4. When the Dolce de Leche is cooked, pour it into 4 bowls to serve.

Nutrition:

- Calories: 91
- Fat: 2.5 g
- Protein 2.2 g

146. CHAMPAGNE ZABAGLIONE

Preparation Time: 21 minutes
Cooking Time: 60 minutes
Serving: 4
Ingredients:

- 4 large egg yolks
- 1/2 cup of superfine sugar
- 1/2 cup of champagne
- 1/2 cup of heavy whipping cream
- 1/2-pint of fresh raspberries

Directions:
1. Preheat your Anova Precision Cooker to 165 °F or 74 °C.
2. Place the eggs in a bowl and slowly whisk in the sugar. Continue to whisk until ingredients become thick. Add the champagne and continue to whisk lightly until you have dissolved the sugar.
3. Place the mixture in a sous vide bag. Then, place the bag in the preheated container. Set your Anova timer for 20 minutes.
4. Meanwhile, prepare an ice bath. Once cooked, put the bag in the ice bath until cold. Whip the cream and fold the whipped cream into the cold zabaglione.
5. Place a layer of the mixture in a glass and then top with some berries. Add another layer of the mixture and top with a couple more berries. Repeat the process with 3 more glasses.
6. Serve immediately

Nutrition:

- Calories: 231
- Fat: 10.3 g
- Protein 3.5 g

147. MEXICAN POT DE CRÈME

Preparation Time: 2 hours 40 minutes
Cooking Time: 30 minutes
Serving: 5
Ingredients:
- 1 cup of heavy whipping cream
- 1/2 cup of whole milk
- 1 cup of bittersweet chocolate, chopped
- 1/2 teaspoon of cinnamon
- 1 tablespoon of sugar
- 3 egg yolks
- 2 teaspoon of cocoa powder
- 1/2 teaspoon of vanilla extract
- 1/8 teaspoon of salt
- flakey sea salt for garnish
- 5 (4-oz) mason jars

Directions:
1. Preheat your Anova Precision Cooker to 180 °F or 82°C. Chop the chocolate and put it in a large bowl with the sugar and cinnamon.
2. Heat a pan on medium heat with cream and milk. Allow the mixture to come to a boil, and then pour it over the chocolate. Let the mixture rest for 5 minutes.
3. While the mixture is resting, whisk together the vanilla, salt, cocoa powder, and eggs.
4. Stir the chocolate mixture. Whisk in the cocoa powder mixture into the chocolate mixture.
5. Pour an equal amount of the mixture into the mason jars. Place the mason jars in your preheated container and set your Anova timer for 30 minutes.
6. When the jars are cooked, place them on top of a kitchen towel on the counter to cool for 20 minutes. Place the cooled jars in the refrigerator for at least 2 hours.
7. Sprinkle the jars with a little sea salt to serve.

Nutrition:
- Calories: 332
- Fat: 22.4 g
- Protein 5.6 g

148. LAVENDER SPICED CRÈME BRULÉE

Preparation Time: 2 hours 20 minutes
Cooking Time: 60 minutes
Serving: 6
Ingredients:

- 8 jumbo egg yolks
- 1/2 cup of sugar plus more for topping
- 1 teaspoon of salt
- 1 teaspoon of culinary lavender
- 2 1/2 cups of heavy whipping cream

Directions:

1. Preheat your Anova Precision Cooker to 176 °F or 80 °C.
2. Combine the eggs, sugar, lavender, and salt in a bowl and whisk them together.
3. Heat the cream on medium heat until simmering.
4. Carefully and slowly, mix the cream into the lavender mixture using a whisk. Otherwise, the eggs will curdle.
5. Strain the ingredients and discard the lavender. Pour an equal amount of the mixture into 6 mason jars. Tighten the lids, so they're finger tight. You don't want to tighten the lids as tight as possible because the trapped air may crack the jars.
6. Place the jars in your preheated container and set your Anova timer for 1 hour.
7. Once cooked, place the jars on a kitchen towel on the counter. Let the jars come down to room temperature.
8. Prepare an ice bath. Put the cooled jars in the ice bath until cold, top the crème Brulée with a layer of sugar and use a kitchen torch to caramelize it. Allow it to harden for 5 minutes
9. Serve immediately.

Nutrition:

- Calories: 321
- Fat: 24.4 g
- Protein 8.5 g

149. CRÈME BRULÉE

Preparation Time: 2 hours 20 minutes
Cooking Time: 60 minutes
Serving: 6
Ingredients:

- 11 egg yolks
- 1 cup of granulated sugar, plus more for dusting
- 3 g of salt
- 600 g of heavy cream
- 6 (6-oz) mason jars

Directions:

1. Preheat your Anova Precision Cooker to 176 °F or 80 °C.
2. Place the eggs, sugar, and salt in a bowl and whisk them together.
3. Carefully and slowly, mix the cream into the egg mixture using a whisk. Otherwise, the eggs will curdle.
4. Strain the new mixture and allow it to rest for 20-30 minutes. The goal is to get rid of all the bubbles. Take off any removing bubbles.
5. Slowly pour an equal amount of the mixture from a low height into the mason jars. You want to make sure you don't create more bubbles.
6. Tighten the lids, so they're finger tight. You don't want to tighten the lids as tight as possible because the trapped air may crack the jars.
7. Place the jars in your preheated container and set your Anova timer for 1 hour.
8. Once cooked, place the jars on a kitchen towel on the counter. Let the jars come down to room temperature.
9. Prepare an ice bath and place the cooled jars in the ice bath until cold.
10. Top the Crème Brulée with a layer of sugar using a sieve and use a kitchen torch to caramelize it. Allow it to harden for 5 minutes
11. Serve immediately.

Nutrition:

- Calories: 444
- Fat: 45.3 g
- Protein 7 g

150. LECHE FLAN

Preparation Time: 21 minutes

Cooking Time: 60 minutes

Serving: 4

Ingredients:

- 3/4 cups of granulated sugar
- 12 egg yolks
- 1 (14-oz can) of condensed milk
- 1 (12-oz can) of evaporated milk
- 1 teaspoon of vanilla extract
- 4 (1/2 pint) mason jars

Directions:

1. Preheat your Anova Precision Cooker to 180 °F or 82 °C.
2. Heat the sugar in a saucepan on medium-high heat. Stir constantly until the sugar melts and turns a caramel color. Pour equal portions of the caramel into the 4 mason jars and allow it cool
3. Lightly mix the remaining ingredients and strain through cheesecloth. Pour an equal amount into the mason jars.
4. Place the jars in the preheated container and set your Anova timer for 2 hours.
5. When the flan is cooked, place the jars on a kitchen towel on the counter. Allow the jars to cool down to room temperature.
6. Place the jars in the refrigerator for at least 2 hours before serving.
7. Serve directly in the jar or remove and put the flan on a plate.

Nutrition:

- Calories: 665
- Fat: 26.6 g
- Protein: 19.9 g

151. CINNAMON CLOVE BANANA BOWLS

Preparation Time: 11 minutes

Cooking Time: 35 minutes

Serving: 6

Ingredients:

- 7 ripe bananas
- 2 cinnamon sticks
- 1-1/4 cup of brown sugar
- 6 cloves, whole

Directions:

1. Preheat your Anova Precision Cooker to 176 °F or 80 °C. Peel the banana and slice it into chunks
2. Combine all the ingredients in a sous vide bag.
3. Place the bag in your preheated container and set your Anova timer for 35 minutes.
4. When the bananas are cooked, place them in 6 bowls and let them cool slightly.
5. Remove the cinnamon and cloves and serve alone or with ice cream.

Nutrition:

- Calories: 241
- Fat: 1.8 g
- Protein 2 g

152. CREAMY SWEET CORN CHEESECAKE

Preparation Time: 31 minutes
Cooking Time: 40 minutes
Serving: 6
Ingredients:

- 1 cup of frozen sweet corn
- 1/2 cup of heavy cream
- 1/2 cup of whole milk
- 4 eggs
- 1 cup of sugar
- 1 tablespoon of lemon juice
- 2 lemon peels
- 1/2 cup of butter
- 3/4 cups of cream cheese
- 3 gingerbread cookies
- 6 (6-oz) mason jars

Directions:

1. Preheat your Anova Precision Cooker to 176 °F or 80 °C. Defrost the corn.
2. Place the first 6 ingredients in a blender and blend at high speed until smooth.
3. Add the mixture and the lemon peels to a sous vide bag.
4. Place the bag in your preheated container and set your Anova timer for 40 minutes.
5. When the mixture is cooked, discard the peels and place the mix back in the blender.
6. Add in the cream cheese and butter and blend on high until smooth. Allow the mixture to cool completely.
7. Pour an equal amount of the mixture in each Mason jar. Crumble up the cookies and top each Mason jar with the crumbs before serving.

Nutrition:

- Calories: 490
- Fat: 33.8 g
- Protein 8 g

153. SWEET CORN CHEESECAKE

Preparation Time: 15 minutes
Cooking Time: 90 minutes
Serving: 5
Ingredients:
- 2 (8-oz) packages of cream cheese
- 100 g of granulated sugar
- 2 g of kosher salt
- 3 whole eggs
- 5 g of vanilla extract
- 130 g of buttermilk, or heavy whipping cream
- 5 (8-oz) mason jars

Directions:
1. Preheat your Anova Precision Cooker to 176 °F or 80 °C. Allow the cream cheese to rise to room temperature.
2. Put the cream cheese, salt, and sugar in a food processor. Process until smooth, making sure you scrape the sides of the bowl throughout to ensure all ingredients are mixed.
3. Put in the eggs and vanilla and follow the same process as last time.
4. While the food processor is running, pour in the buttermilk. Continue to process until smooth. Strain the mixture through a fine-mesh sieve for the smoothest texture. Pour an equal amount of mixture into each jar.
5. Tighten the lids, so they're finger tight but not fully airtight to prevent cracking of the jars.
6. Put the jars in your preheated container and set your Anova timer for 90 minutes.
7. When the cheesecake is cooked, place the jars on a kitchen towel on the counter. Let the jars come to room temperature. Refrigerate overnight.
8. Serve as is or with your favorite toppings.

Nutrition:
- Calories: 443
- Fat: 34.5 g
- Protein 11 g

154. BANANAS FOSTER

Preparation Time: 15 minutes
Cooking Time: 26 minutes
Serving: 2
Ingredients:
- 2 tablespoons of dark rum
- 4 tablespoons of butter
- 1 teaspoon of vanilla
- 1/2 cup of brown sugar
- 2 bananas
- 1 teaspoon of cinnamon
- 2 scoops of vanilla ice cream

Directions:
1. Preheat your Anova Precision Cooker to 145 °F or 63 °C. Peel and cut the bananas into 1-inch pieces.
2. Place the vanilla, butter, brown sugar, and rum in a pan over high heat. Bring the mixture to a boil and remove it from heat.
3. Season the bananas with cinnamon and put them in the bag of your choice with 3 tablespoons of sauce.
4. Place the bag in your preheated container and set your Anova timer for 25 minutes.
5. When the bananas are cooked, plate them with a scoop of vanilla ice cream and top with the remaining sauce.
6. Serve immediately.

Nutrition:
- Calories: 722
- Fat: 40.4 g
- Protein 5.4 g

155. MAPLE RAISIN RICE PUDDING WITH GINGER

Preparation Time: 6 minutes
Cooking Time: 2 hours
Serving: 8
Ingredients:
- 3 cups of skim milk
- 2 tablespoon of butter
- 2 cups of Arborio rice
- 1/2 cup of golden raisins
- 1/2 cup of maple syrup
- 2 teaspoon of ground cinnamon
- 1/2 teaspoon of ground ginger

Directions:
1. Preheat your Anova Precision Cooker to 180 °F or 82 °C.
2. Put all the ingredients in a sous vide bag and place the bag in your preheated container, and set your Anova timer for 2 hours.
3. Once cooked, place equal portions in 8 bowls.
4. Top each bowl with a little extra cinnamon to serve.

Nutrition:
- Calories: 311
- Fat: 3.2 g
- Protein 6.5 g

CONCLUSION

I hope you enjoyed reading this cookbook. Sous Vide is truly an artful skill that is worth mastering. If it is your first time, don't fear to fail, the results you want to achieve. You will definitely get better while getting experience with this cookbook! The key is patience, the right information, and consistency.

The Sous-vide method is all about the simplicity through perfect texture and exquisite aroma of your food. My deepest desire is to create a cookbook that will transform your everyday recipes into a rich heavenly meal that will gather your family around the table and create some precious memories.

The term Sous Vide is derived from the French language, meaning "under vacuum." It is pronounced as Sue-Veed. Sous vide cooking takes a different and unique approach to certain types of food. As the term 'under vacuum' implies, the technique is employed by cooking food under vacuum. Since this process seems far different from all the conventional forms of cooking, it is often thought of as being too difficult. Luckily, various electric sous vide cookers are now available on the market, which ensures perfect sous vide cooking.

Well, one great advantage of using a sous vide cooker is that it gives a bigger cooking window. Since the sous vide machine cooks on relatively low heat and even temperatures, it hardly overcooks the food if left unchecked for 2-3 hours over the set cooking time. With the rise of recent sous vide technology, now that window of error is also shut closed as the sous vide machines beep or indicate in some other way that the food is ready.

Adopting sous vide cooking techniques to your kitchen doesn't just make you a better chef. It provides many benefits that you'll enjoy.

For one, cooking with sous vide allows you to retain the nutrients in the food that would normally be lost or damaged through traditional cooking methods. In addition to this, your cutlery and appliances will last longer because they won't get as hot during normal use.

The best part is that sous vide cooking is a great way to prepare your food perfectly every time!

Experiment regularly, and soon you will become an expert in Sous Vide cooking. The 300+ recipes in this book give you a wide variety to experiment with your cooking.

Start trying out the sous vide cooking method for yourself. This cooking method is simple to work with, and you really only need a few supplies to get it all started. As long as you take the essential steps, you will be able to create a delicious meal that is going to make people love your cooking.

Don't worry if you still feel a little cautious about trying a new form of cooking. However, you should never allow your fears to stop you from leaping into a better world of cooking and eating. Trust me; once you start to cook Sous Vide, you will find yourself eating healthier, making meal plans, and enjoying your time in the kitchen. This is especially true on those hot and humid days when you don't feel like being in the kitchen cooking or going out because it's all too hot.

Don't wait another day to try Sous Vide cooking. It is one of the best ways to cook and reheat your food. Furthermore, you can keep some foods, such as meats, vacuumed sealed in your freezer for up to a year. Enjoy cooking!

Made in the USA
Monee, IL
22 July 2021